Reimagining Mission from Urban Places

Reimagining Mission From Urban Places

Missional Pastoral Care

Anna Ruddick

scm press

© Anna Ruddick 2020

Published in 2020 by SCM Press
Editorial office
3rd Floor, Invicta House,
108–114 Golden Lane,
London EC1Y 0TG, UK
www.scmpress.co.uk

SCM Press is an imprint of Hymns Ancient & Modern Ltd
(a registered charity)

H
Y
M Ancient
N &Modern
S

Hymns Ancient & Modern® is a registered trademark of
Hymns Ancient & Modern Ltd
13A Hellesdon Park Road, Norwich,
Norfolk NR6 5DR, UK

British Library Cataloguing in Publication data

A catalogue record for this book is available
from the British Library

ISBN 978 0 334 05865 6
Illustrations by www.mattdoherty.co.uk
Cover image © www.katylunsford.com

Typeset by Manila Typesetting Company
Printed and bound by
CPI Group (UK) Ltd

Contents

Acknowledgements

It feels like time for this book; and, equally, this is a book of its time. A particular moment within British evangelicalism created the Eden Network, alongside other incarnational mission initiatives. Since then, many courageous and dedicated Christians have joined Eden teams and have committed themselves to missional living in communities described as marginalized. This research belongs to them and to their neighbours as much as to me. It arises primarily from the urban community members and team members I interviewed and I have lived and worked alongside. I am immensely grateful to them for their wisdom, honesty and creativity, without which there would be nothing to say.

I am not alone in responding to this cultural and theological moment. I have been challenged and encouraged by friends and colleagues on similar journeys as we articulate some complementary shifts from our different standpoints, and for each of their unique gifts I am grateful.

In the process of re-storying a doctoral thesis for a general readership I have benefited hugely from friends, family and colleagues who have read drafts, listened and offered their reflections. Thank you!

Finally, my love and gratitude go to Andrew Ruddick, an incisive editor and true encourager. I am so glad to be able to share this adventure with you!

I

Reality is Good Enough

> When people join in with you and support the cause that you both believe in and it's like, wow, this is really collaborative and I never expected it to be like this . . . I always thought it would be, you know, like our team getting together behind our vision and making it happen . . . And, you know, maybe I expect to be great and stooping, you know, when really it's about another person helping me and changing me and humbling me in the process and helping me realize, oh my goodness what a gift, what a gift that that person wants to give to me, how beautiful is that! (Mission team member, Greater Manchester)

These words are the reflections of an evangelical Christian in his twenties who had relocated to an urban community and had been living there for four years. He is not a church leader or a professional mission practitioner in any way. Instead he has sought to share his day-to-day life with the people of his community, hoping to share his faith in the midst of it all. In these few words he articulates the gift that this choice has been to him, and also the challenge. It has led to unexpected outcomes, and he has been changed in the process.

'Missional pastoral care' is the name I have given to an intentional form of missional living shaped by seven elements: being among people who are different, living locally, being available, taking practical action, long-term commitment, consistency and love.

Mission is usually seen as what Christians do among people *before* these people become Christians. It is often characterized as edgy and exciting, requiring entrepreneurial leadership and great communication skills, whereas pastoral care is perceived to be what happens within the Church, among existing Christians. It is characterized as quieter and more introverted, mainly concerned with helping people through personal problems. Pastoral care can easily be sidelined, particularly in strongly activist and mission-orientated contexts, while we all 'get out there' on mission. I appreciate these are caricatures, but ones that perhaps many of us recognize.

But among the incarnational mission teams of the Eden Network these categories have begun to seem less clear. Their ministry involves supporting and caring for vulnerable people over the long term, without this being seen as a means to the end of evangelism. It does include faith-sharing but is not focused primarily on evangelism; and while it can lead to conversion, this is not the sole aim. Members of Eden teams understand their work as mission, although in it there are patterns that echo pastoral care. So these two vocations, which often seem so different, are brought together in 'missional pastoral care', a way of life that enacts the mission of God in three ways: by holistically sharing our lives (for the common good) with those we once thought of as 'other'; by talking about our life stories, including faith stories; and by engaging in a process of reshaping our world views, leading to life change.

This book is an account of mission in marginal communities: the experiences of Christians involved in mission and the urban community members they got to know. In their often unheard reflections we find a changed mission, and a changing evangelicalism. Whatever they may have expected it to be, mission turns out to be about recognizing the personhood of people who we assume are 'other' to us. It is about leaning into the discomfort of vulnerability and about celebrating the flourishing that comes when we do. Mission, as it turns out, has something in common with pastoral care – blurring the lines between mission and discipleship, between the Christian on mission and non-Christians in a community. In the end we discover that God is on mission and that mission is to us all, whether we name ourselves Christian or not. The invitation is to be open to God's mission in our lives as Christians as a fundamental part of our joining with God in mission in our world.

My questions about mission, the way people change and the language we use to describe it came about through my work for the Eden Network over a period of nine years. The Eden Network is an initiative of The Message Trust, a Christian mission organization based in Manchester and working nationally and internationally. It engages in incarnational urban mission, developing partnerships with local churches or church planting denominations and recruiting teams of Christians to relocate into communities identified, using government statistics, as among the most deprived in the country.[1]

'Missional pastoral care' is the result of many conversations, observations and much grappling. Specifically, it is the result of a programme of doctoral research, which began in response to my work supporting Eden team members, and with the starting question: 'What does it take to change a life in an urban community?' It seemed evident to me that God is at work in the experiences of Eden teams and in the urban communities that they inhabit. My hope was to find out *how* God is at work, and that meant unravelling many of my own assumptions and the corporate narratives of the Network. Now, working as a community theologian in a range of different contexts, I have found that the learnings of Eden team members and urban community members offer a rich source of theological reflection for Christian mission. This is not a book about the Eden Network, nor is it my intention to offer an evaluation of incarnational urban mission models. Rather, Eden's gift was (and still is) to provide a way for ordinary evangelical Christians to become neighbours and build relationships in marginal communities. This book is about what happens when they do and what it can teach us about God, ourselves and the task of mission in twenty-first-century British society.

The insights shared here have arisen within the context of urban ministry, and all of the people mentioned live in communities that experience poverty and marginalization. While this is a book about ministry and mission in urban places, it is also *not* about ministry and mission in urban places. It is about relationships in mission – how they work, what makes them life-giving and how we understand them to be fruitful. Writing about mission and ministry in urban contexts is important, but here I am doing something different. I am writing about mission and ministry *from* experiences in urban contexts. Having spent the last 14 years listening to and reflecting with people involved in urban ministry, and having lived in marginalized communities myself for half of that time, I believe that the urban is a place of encounter with God, with ourselves and with those we consider to be 'other'. When people all around us are living with the precariousness of low incomes, inadequate financial or relational safety nets, poverty of expectation and the disdain of wider society, life is raw. Emotions run near the surface and the barrier between small talk and places of deep pain is tissue thin. The injustices of marginalization in our society cannot be ignored; however, in the communities experiencing this injustice there is great gift and strength. Mission at the margins is, if we have eyes to see it, a place of new life, in which our ideas about God, ourselves and the way the world works can be challenged and reshaped. By writing *from* urban experience rather than *about* urban experience, I will try to offer some of that gift to people in a wide variety of mission contexts. For those engaged in urban mission, many of these ideas may not feel new, or may resonate deeply with your experience. When I talk about my work with practitioners the response is often 'Yes, this is what we do!' It is also frequently followed by 'Help me explain this to my manager/church.' You may find that this research provides new language to help you frame what you do or that it sets your experiences in a wider theological or socio-psychological context. For others in non-urban contexts it might invite you to be attentive to your own inherited theological narratives; to ask 'What is reality in my mission and am I learning from it?'; and to question the nature of your missional relationships and your hopes for them. So what is this wisdom *from* the urban?

You are enough! . . . and reality is good enough

You are enough! This profoundly countercultural suggestion is one of the most healing things we can ever hear. A surprising number of people – cheered on by a consumer, hyper-capitalist society in which success is equated to growth, and efficient fixing of life's challenges is prized above all – struggle to believe this simple truth: that we, as we are, are enough (Brown, 2013). I think that the struggle for self-acceptance that pervades many of our interior lives is also worked out in our mission, given a distinct flavour by a particular understanding of who God is and how God works in the world.

My experience and research alongside those who have intentionally adopted missional lifestyles and those they have met in their communities suggests that many struggle to accept their mission for what it is. Mission practitioners can feel inadequate in the face of theological narratives, often framed in biblical language, of what mission should be. For example, perhaps you are involved in mission as part of a church that carries an expectation of coming revival. What if that revival is understood by church leadership and members to be a work of the Holy Spirit in which large numbers of people will suddenly be convicted of their sin, repent and flood into the church? That's an amazing hope, and one that has been held by many congregations throughout the twentieth century since the well-publicized revivals in Wales, the Hebrides and beyond. So you are involved in mission, longing to see people come to faith, and this story of revival gives you a certain expectation of what that will look like. But what if your mission seems completely different from that revival narrative? Maybe only a few people come to faith over a number of years, and they come falteringly, not finding church an easy place to be. You may find yourself feeling inadequate in your mission, asking 'What am I doing wrong, why is the reality falling so far short of my expectation?'

Throughout evangelical history (the last 300 years or so), this tension between expectation and reality has led to some interesting shifts in emphasis. It tends to swing, as many cultural trends do, from one extreme to another. In the nineteenth century, Victorian evangelicals were great activists in philanthropy, working hard for social change – think of the campaigns against slavery, the early Salvation Army and Christian business owners – such as the Rowntrees – seeking to reshape society. These efforts had a huge impact, radically changing the world; but not everyone was converted, or saved from poverty, or stopped from drinking to excess. Many evangelical Christians felt disappointed by this and the emphasis shifted from their activism to the belief that social transformation could only happen at God's initiative. So the pendulum swung towards prayer and personal devotion; people felt that all their efforts hadn't been enough, and that if they just sought God's presence then God would come and change the world. I have painted this mini-history in very broad brush strokes but I hope it gives you a sense that this tussle between expectations and reality is not new, and it impacts the development of our faith as individuals and our faith traditions. However, there is always an opportunity to step back, acknowledge the pattern of effort, disappointment, retreat, then renew effort and begin to ask different questions. *What is actually happening in the mission experiences that we deem inadequate? Are we missing something? Is there a different way?* I believe that there is, and my intention is to say to you, as I have to many mission practitioners before you, that you are enough, and in your mission *reality* is enough!

But how do we know what mission is? And how do we know what we should expect to see as the result of our mission?

The Bible is the obvious starting point, certainly for me with my broadly evangelical Christian background. It seems simple. We read the Bible, we see that mission is about the birth and growth of the Church, people coming to know Jesus and beginning to participate in communities of Christians who live differently from those around them. For those from other Christian traditions there might be a different starting point – the lives of the saints, the stories of heroic struggles for social justice and liberation from across the globe. Wherever you start, what is often missed is just how filtered these narratives are; and how coloured they are by our own cultural lenses – our time, place and season.

Evangelical Christians living intentionally missional life-styles bring a missional narrative with them to the task. This narrative comes from their Christian experiences to date: from church, Christian festivals and conferences, books, friends and leaders. But often their experiences don't fit with that inherited narrative. What they encounter in mission – real relationships with real people who don't claim to be Christians – challenges their expectations of what mission is and how God works. As a result, they can be vulnerable to disappointment, disillusion-ment, or retreating to a safe distance, attempting to protect themselves from the dissonance. When we recognize God at work in our mission and try to set aside our inherited assump-tions in order to understand what God is doing, we find a different perspective. The story I want to tell is that mission doesn't work the way we think it does. In reality, it works through making and remaking meaning, happening in shared life. It is not something we do to others for God but something that God is doing in the world, including in us.

Transformation – what does it really mean?

It's like making an egg.
Like making an egg?
Yeah.
What do you mean?
'Cos you watch it go from just the white and the yolk into an actually fully formed egg.
OK?
You watch it transform.
Oh, like boiled do you mean, and harden?
Yeah.

I asked Suzy, a 19-year-old from Greater Manchester, what she thought transformation was and this was her reply. I think it illustrates the slipperiness of this much-used word.

If you ask a Christian leader, either in church or in a Christian mission or charitable organization, what they want to see as the result of their ministry and mission, it's likely that the word 'transformation' will crop up in the first few sentences. Some prioritize the individual ('seeing lives transformed') whereas others take a more community or regional perspective ('social transformation'). Still others combine the two, aiming for the cumulative effect of manageable, personal mission: 'transforming our world, one person at a time'. The language of transformation is everywhere. When I started this research it was this word that fascinated me. For many years, and during my employment with the Eden Network, their strapline was 'transforming communities from the inside out'. There it was, our aim: transformation. I spent a lot of time talking about transformation and trying to define it. Starting with Suzy's egg illustration, transformation seems to be about change; and set in the context in which most Christians use the term, it's about positive change. Many people link it to ideas of metamorphosis to describe a seismic change in a person or situation – something more dramatic than a small-scale, ordinary change of opinion or a new habit. Before long the beginning of Romans 12 comes into view. In verse 2 Paul says 'Do not conform to the pattern of this world, but be transformed by the renewing of your mind. Then you will be able to test and approve what God's will is – his good, pleasing and perfect will' (Rom. 12.2, NIV). His emphasis on patterns and the mind in this verse is really interesting. It resonates with what I found in my research about how people change, but more of that later.

'Transformation' is a word that describes a process of positive change more than a particular outcome. The expected outcomes differ depending on who is using the word. For example, a local council talking about a community initiative might say that its aim is to transform the community. A church leader might do the same. But it's likely that they do not mean exactly the same thing.

Transformation language acts as a kind of code, what sociologists describe as a 'discourse' (Garnett et al., 2007, pp. 160–6). When a church has the word 'transformation' in its mission statement, that word is filled with meaning. It does not simply refer to positive change, but instead refers to particular kinds of changes that are perceived by that church to be positive and desirable, such as conversion – maybe, for example, no longer smoking dope every weekend – or feeling more joyful in daily life. So the people within that church might talk together about transformation and the word becomes a kind of shared shorthand for the changes they want to see in the world. When language becomes a 'discourse' in this way it is not only used by groups to describe their activities, it also becomes a part of the way the group interprets situations around them, 'the position from which . . . we see the world' (Garnett, et al., 2007, pp. 160–6). This means that members of the group are tuned in to look for their particular version of transformation (or the lack of it) as they experience the world, and evaluate and interpret other people, organizations or experiences in terms of their role in, or demonstration of, that transformation.

Coded language is extremely useful, as it creates shared understandings and enables belonging to grow between individuals and different groups. Transformation discourse is intelligible to a wide variety of people and in fact is used by a huge variety of different organizations, including churches, other religious groups, statutory agencies and non-religious charitable organizations. In each of the different contexts in which the word 'transformation' is used it is filled with meaning specific to that group or organization. But by using the discourse of transformation, specific groups can feel a sense of unity and shared purpose with a whole range of different parties.

It is not surprising that transformation language has become so ubiquitous. The shifts in our society over the last 100 years or so have moved us firmly into religious and cultural pluralism. Churches are recognizing that their truth claims must be offered with gentleness and respect to a society in which different versions of truth abound. Transformation is friendlier, less exclusive language than 'salvation', for example. Another reason for the strength of this discourse is the resurgence, particularly within evangelical churches, of social and community engagement throughout the later twentieth century and into the twenty-first. Transformation can include both the desire for individual change in conversion and for community change in the systemic 'kingdom coming'. In our current context of economic austerity there are enormous social challenges in our country and a willingness from government (rightly or wrongly) to allow religious groups to plug gaps in welfare provision. When engaging with systemic issues in communities such as health, education, addiction or housing, church congregations have sought a language that could enable different agencies to understand their aims and enter into partnership.

A final benefit of transformation discourse is precisely that its meaning can be fluid. It offers positive, catch-all language to talk about aims and outcomes while the nature of those outcomes is as yet emerging. Given our situation of rapid social and cultural change, churches are increasingly aware that there is no more business as usual. Movements such as Emerging Church, Fresh Expressions and Pioneer ministry draw on themes of creativity and entrepreneurship to inform the development of new models of mission and ministry in uncharted cultural territories. For such innovations, the flexibility of transformation language allows wider denominations or church hierarchies to understand their aims and hear about outcomes in ways that can be understood, even while new developments are as yet uncertain.

Transformation language is a pragmatic discourse that is meaningful because it is useful as a positive way to articulate ambitions for creating positive change in the world (Swinton and Pattison, 2010, p. 226). Despite its benefits, I think that over-reliance on transformation discourse, particularly in relation to mission, is problematic. What is left unsaid when the language of transformation is used to enable partnership or clarify emerging innovation? 'Transformation' acts as shorthand for positive changes that an individual or group wishes to see in the world. The difficulty arises when the 'longhand' or specific aspirations of a group are not reflected on or named.

In relation to partnership, it is easy to see (and many leaders will have experienced this) how shared action between groups can begin with energy and optimism, but become difficult when what actually happens as a result of the work begins to highlight the differences between the partners. For example, a common experience for youth workers is that their churches initiate youthwork, longing to see the lives of young people transformed. So far so good. The youth worker gets going, building relationships and beginning to see signs of progress. However, the congregation are expecting transformation to look like young people coming to church on Sunday morning, 'sensibly' dressed and knowing roughly when to listen and when to interact throughout the service. The youth worker may become disillusioned when their 'successes' are not recognized by the church as they don't fit these rather narrow criteria for 'transformation'. This may seem a cliché but these patterns are played out to varying degrees over different issues in many, if not most, churches.

The other challenge to transformation language is in relation to innovation. When it is used to describe the outcomes of new and innovative mission activity, it can prevent the necessary reflection and learning from experience that needs to take place. It seems reasonable that if new emergent models of ministry are being developed, the outcomes of such ministry might also be unexpected. However, innovation is often really concerned with finding new, better ways to achieve the same things. When transformation is used to describe outcomes and there is no openness to reflect on what is actually happening as a result of an innovative approach to mission, then practitioners can become disillusioned and hierarchies disappointed. Worst of all, everyone misses the opportunity to learn and grow, even to encounter God, through their innovation.

Disillusionment, confusion and failure

I interviewed Sally, a mission team member who, at the time of our conversation, had been a part of Eden for ten years. She talked about the changes she hoped to see from her ministry:

> I don't know, it's a hard . . . I think your expectation is different, isn't it, so you maybe have a hope that they're just

totally going to understand everything that you're telling them and they're just going to wake up tomorrow morning and they'll be praying in tongues and laying on hands and healing people and everything like that but actually in reality my faith is just not big enough to believe for that so I'll just be happy for somebody who decides not to have a glass of wine for breakfast . . .

Sally's words demonstrate the difficulties that arise when mission practitioners are not enabled to reflect deeply on their experiences, their theology and their hopes in ministry. She wants to see immediate and radical life change among the people of her community, and she describes a particular set of positive changes that she has inherited from her experiences of church and theological tradition, and which she associates with transformation. Sally's experience of urban ministry has led her to adjust her expectations, but that process is not comfortable or easy. She describes it as not having enough faith. In her confusion as to why the changes she hoped for have not happened, she takes on the responsibility herself, concluding that 'my faith is just not big enough'. For Sally, there is a sense in which if she could increase her faith to 'believe for more', then perhaps more would be possible. Although she has found that she can be happy with someone simply choosing cereal rather than wine for breakfast – a good aspiration for us all I think! – such language suggests feelings of inadequacy and failure. These are themes that have been consistently and uncomfortably present in my work with mission practitioners.

The ministry of Eden teams had a clearly articulated model, and 'transformation' as its expected outcome; but this was becoming increasingly problematic as their experiences ceased to reflect their aims and inherited paradigms. Creating spaces for members of Eden teams to gather was a central priority for the Eden Network and a key aspect of my role there. Facilitating these events across the country, I spent time listening to their reflections. Volunteers join Eden with an inherited theology that shapes the expectations they have for their urban ministry. For the majority, this means a hope that they will see people in their communities 'receive salvation' and begin to lead a radically different lifestyle. Over the years of my involvement with Eden, team members described feeling the tension between this expectation and the reality of their experience. At times, a strongly evangelistic emphasis has led to focusing primarily on celebrating stories of conversion, which, for many Eden teams, were less frequent than they had anticipated. This created unease, a fear that they were doing something wrong.

Encouraging and supporting mission practitioners is a vital task in any organization, and the Eden Network worked hard to do this well, including providing space to begin exploring the questions that their ministry was raising for team members. It was clear that Eden teams were not seeing the kinds of outcomes that they expected. However, they *were* seeing significant things happening in their communities; they were just *different* things from those anticipated. Their struggles were about reconciling reality with their expectations. One team member I interviewed in 2010 said: 'We hadn't expected to be close enough to see the real quality of the good stuff that's happened . . . that's been one of the real blessings, the detail of what God's been doing in the ones and twos really' (Thompson, 2012, p. 54).

This also resonated with my own experience of living in an urban community. In my local church, Sunday gatherings were very diverse and often chaotic, including people with a wide variety of perspectives on faith. It seemed that for some of these people, 'church' was something to do, somewhere to bring their children and a place of belonging, but that the shared activities of worship were perceived as irrelevant or unnecessary. On one occasion I facilitated us acting out the parable of the Pharisee and the tax collector in Luke 18. Some of the more disengaged members of the group volunteered to participate and one man, in his twenties, read the lines of the tax collector. I asked him to share how he felt putting himself in the shoes of the tax collector, and he spoke movingly about identifying with a sense of being looked down on by wider society. As we began to talk about the experience in small groups, this man, previously on the fringe of the gathering, became a leader, with a group around him keen to talk about how they viewed themselves in the passage. I found this transition a powerful provocation. This man did not fit with many of my expectations for leadership or participation in church life, although God was clearly at work in him, and through him in others. Incidents such as these challenged me and roused my curiosity; something significant was happening but I was unable to find the language for it. Through these experiences I became convinced that rather than 'doing something wrong', Eden teams were doing something profoundly right; we had just not quite understood what it was. While we began to share our questions as a Network, we didn't yet have the theological and practical tools to see what was emerging in the practice of Eden teams.

Learning from the margins

I have described this research as learning from, rather than about, the urban; and the experiences of confusion and feelings of failure articulated above are, I believe, a foundational point of connection between traditional associations with the 'urban' and missional practice. Both are places of marginality – being or feeling left out – not in sync with the comfortable, well-resourced and socially acceptable mainstream.

The static inner city or outer estate, which has traditionally been the focus of urban mission, is now complicated by gentrification and development on one side and transient and precarious low-income gig economy workers and refugee communities on the other. Entrenched and generational poverty still exists in some communities and there are the additional challenges of adapting to religious and cultural diversity. Experiencing the sharp end of austerity in restricted access to housing and other public services leads to disenfranchised communities. The theologian Chris Baker argues that the combination of global forces, hyper-mobility and post-colonial culture creates contested space and marginalization, people who are unable to participate in the consumer-orientated, entertainment-focused and market-driven 'city-lite' (2009, pp. 35–41). These changes mean that many more churches are now in close proximity to poverty, evidenced by the profusion of foodbanks and night shelters across the country. Poverty is now diffuse, rather than being solely concentrated in urban estates or rural communities; deprivation is dispersed right across the UK, and is found to some degree within most communities.

This means that addressing poverty is not the sole proviso of urban ministry and that urban ministry is not necessarily always ministry among those struggling against poverty.[2] If most churches are encountering poverty and urban spaces are mixed, including gentrified and gated communities alongside long-term residents and transient communities, what does urban now mean? I, along with others such as the urban theologian Mike Pears, are increasingly using the language of marginality as a more precise description than urban, and in this book I use both, as the communities I studied are both urban in their built environment and marginalized. Speaking of mission 'at the margins' usefully combines 'both geographical and social exclusion' and 'physical poverty and multiple forms of deprivation' (Pears, 2016, p. 37). It more fully accounts for the fluid and hybrid nature of our communities and ensures that attention to poverty and injustice is not restricted to cities or outer estates.

Reflecting on marginalization also highlights inequality in society. The margins are the places and communities of those who have been left out, who are often demonized and judged by those with little understanding of their experience. Many Christians, including myself and the majority of church leaders, are part of the mainstream, not the margins – well-educated, with resources and networks of friends and family to support them, able, with their smartphones and good coffee, to participate to some extent in our consumer culture.

In the years that I have lived and worked in, among and around marginalized communities, the people that I have met and shared life with have been a great gift to me. One of the most significant things they have given me has been the opportunity to acknowledge my own brokenness, the aspects of myself that I would rather marginalize, judge or deny. Middle-class communities and churches often struggle with perfectionism; desiring to achieve the perfect careers, food, home, children and lifestyle, we polish ourselves up to present ourselves to others, even to God. Authenticity in church also has respectable limits; there are boundaried times and places for tears, and by and large they are respected. In marginal places people, often by necessity, wear their vulnerability on the outside. Their circumstances are such that pretending it's all OK is much harder – or actually impossible. I have learnt from people who are left out in our society that God loves us in our vulnerability and brokenness, that he comes alongside us in the mess of our lives, accepting the parts of ourselves that we deem unacceptable. Learning from the margins is to learn that God calls us to embrace and accept ourselves in our brokenness and vulnerability, as God accepts us. This is revolutionary for a Church that is often so keen to be seen as attractive, as having it all together, as the place to find the answers.

The confusing and at times disappointing experiences of mission practitioners expose their vulnerability and brokenness and, in doing so, they open the way for us to encounter God's radical acceptance – but only if we lean into the discomfort and learn from it. Transformation language, despite creating space in which to experiment and providing reassurance in uncertainty, can become unhelpful when attention is not given to understanding the experiences that lie beneath such discourse. Furthermore, our experiences in marginal places offer us an opportunity to encounter God in our own brokenness. So it seems necessary to set our ideas of transformation aside for a while and instead open ourselves to ask the deeper and more vulnerable question: *What is really going on?*

Getting to reality

Who defines ministry? Often it is the denominations and organizations who plan and recruit for ministry who develop models, drawing on theology and their experience. Only in more pioneering contexts do practitioners conducting ministry begin to define their work, and rarely are the so-called 'recipients' of that ministry given the opportunity to offer their perspective. In order to get beyond the rhetoric of transformation and find out what was really happening in the ministry of Eden teams, it seemed important to hear from team members and urban community members themselves; for the reality of mission and ministry to be defined from the ground up. But articulating something new is not always easy.

> This is the dimension of being embedded in the stories of a community and of responding to the expectations of the people around us. We cannot tell whichever story we like but have to respond to what those around us consider a legitimate story. In doing so, we follow the narrative models or canonical stories provided by the community in which we live. (Ganzevoort, 2010, p. 335)

These words from the practical theologian Ruard Ganzevoort resonate deeply with my sense that there seemed to be a story being enacted among Eden teams that was not articulated because the 'legitimate story' of the Eden Network community was something slightly different. This is not to say that there wasn't openness within Eden to hear the new narrative, but in a strongly activist movement it can be difficult to find ways to go deeper in reflection and see what was previously unforeseen. Our understanding of what is happening (that is, the story or narrative we tell of events) is shaped not only by the events and experiences themselves, but also by what others around us are expecting to hear. The construction of narratives, and therefore what those stories mean, is always done in relationship with others; the audience, as well as the narrator, shape the story.

My aim has been to try to peel away these layers: to understand what kinds of expectations were shaping the stories team members told about their mission experiences and also to glimpse the substance of their activity as distinct from the stories they told about it. This was a journey for me too. As a member of the national team for Eden, I was a part of telling the stories of Eden teams and was as much immersed in the narratives of the organization, and our particularly evangelical bit of the Christian tradition, as anyone. The task of research became to see missional experiences with fresh eyes and listen in a different way.

To enable this I drew on Practical Theology as a conceptual framework and used qualitative and ethnographic research methods. Throughout 2012 I conducted 16 life-story interviews, seven with Eden team members and nine with urban community members who knew Eden team members locally. My interviewees represented 16 different Eden neighbourhoods across Manchester, Greater Manchester, Yorkshire and the North East. To ensure their anonymity I have given each a pseudonym and limited the amount of personal detail given for each participant. As an insider myself, my professional and personal experience of the Eden Network and its ministry practices became participant observation in the research (Coghlan and Brannick, 2005, pp. 61–3). It is important to say that this piece of research offers a largely white perspective on mission in marginal places. As a white British woman myself and with the majority of my participants, both Eden team members and community members, also white British, it offers a partial view of mission and marginality, the limitations of which I do not take lightly.[3]

All research raises a range of ethical and practical questions and there are a number of different possible approaches. I have outlined my methodology in much more detail in the Appendix, 'Practical Theological Research' on page 200. If you are interested in the research process, or you have questions about the validity of this kind of research, then take a look at the Appendix before reading any further.

Missional pastoral care has emerged from the stories of my two groups of participants, team members and community members; but they had very different starting points in their missional relationships. Team members had relocated from different parts of the country, motivated by a sense that God was calling them to join the Eden Network. They had settled in their urban communities and life had unfolded there; Michael,

Louise and Adam had each married and become parents since joining Eden:

> If you're moving into the area you're actually making a statement, first that you love the area that you're prepared to move into . . . you're not just seeing it as a project you're seeing it as a place where you want to live, make friends and it's not just a place to make change, it's a place where you want to do life. (Adam)

Team members all gave significant time to building relationships and getting involved in their local neighbourhood. As James described: 'We're not perfect but you know we're honest and we're alongside them and I think what Eden does is force you to open your whole life to the community.' Hannah, Sally, Dan and James worked in professions that took them outside of their community for much of the week, whereas Michael, Louise and Adam worked locally.

The community members I interviewed were more diverse in terms of age and life experience, from 16-year-old Jess and Jack, to Margaret and Helen, who are mums in their forties. They had all met Eden team members in the course of their everyday lives but, while for the Eden teams engagement was intentional, for community members it was just what had happened. Margaret described getting to know one of the Eden team at the school gate, whereas David was discovered by a team member in the back garden of an abandoned house. Margaret and Helen both had an inclination towards faith before meeting the team:

> [When] I was a kid I always used to think who is God and I always used to think I know that there's something there but what? . . . d'y'know what I mean? I always believed in God but I wanted to know what is God? (Helen)

David, Jack, Clare, Kevin and Suzy had adopted faith to varying degrees since meeting the Eden team, while Paul and Jess felt it was not for them. They all shared the depth of friendship they had established with Eden team members and the ways it had shaped their lives. Kevin said of one team member: 'I am dead open to [him], you know, 'cos we got a good relationship together, a good friendship and stuff.'

In order to understand these relationships we need to listen – and not just to the Christian practitioners of mission, but to the people they meet. The people who they 'do mission to' don't see this as a task at all and they may not have a particular theological narrative shaping their expectations. But perhaps God is at work in them; they might be able to help us understand our mission, even to come to terms with its reality beyond the rhetoric of transformation, and we may find that reality is better than we ever imagined! Maybe in the case of mission, rather than asking for the gloss of transformation stories, God offers us change, in all of us, including those who call themselves Christian and those who don't; maybe God is offering us grace, and the kingdom.

So what can we learn from reality?

My journey of listening, reflecting and learning is still very much ongoing and I'm sure it will never stop. Nevertheless, here I present the results of a particular phase of listening, which I hope will be helpful to those involved in mission in any context. As I have sought to see the real stuff of mission beneath the expectation and rhetoric, what has emerged is an understanding of mission as having our ways of seeing the world reshaped, and missional pastoral care as a way of living this out in a community.

Mission as meaning-making

Mission is often conceived as the Church taking a message of God's love and power to those outside the Church. It's seen as a task of communication *from* Christians *to* non-Christians, albeit not always in words. But these missional experiences show that mission seems to be less about communication and more about making meaning: changing how we understand ourselves, God and the world. Communicating new information in words and practical actions is just one aspect of the process of meaning-making. What is more, this isn't just happening for non-Christians. Christians engaged in mission are also having their ideas and beliefs challenged and changed, and they attribute this to God at work. So mission becomes God's activity (as *missio Dei*) towards the whole world – those who profess to be Christians and those who don't. It is God's action in challenging and reshaping the ways we see ourselves, others and God, towards an end that might best be described as *shalom*.

Missional pastoral care

Missional pastoral care is a way of life that seeks to share in this mission of God by participating in communities who have been marginalized, developing significant and mutual relationships with people with an eye on the common good. These relationships involve sharing our stories – the way we see the world – and listening to the stories of our neighbours and friends in order to learn from one another. Through this process, both Christians-on-mission and urban community members are changed.

In the chapters that follow we will see how mission and pastoral care come together as we explore the idea of meaning-making as the essence of God's mission, and the ways that this is expressed in the lives of team and community members in marginalized urban neighbourhoods. Chapter 2 starts to explore the reality of mission by looking more closely at how life change happens. Insights from psychology and pastoral care, alongside the stories of my participants, illustrate the way that humans structure reality in narrative world views and how these may be changed and shaped over time through meaning-making in 'parabolic' relationships. Chapter 3 explores what missional pastoral care looks and feels like through seven components: difference, locality, availability, practicality, long-term commitment, consistency and love. It names some practical challenges, such as boundaries and sustainability, and addresses the imbalances of power that are inherent in relocation-based models of mission. Chapter 4 deals with the question of 'success', looking at the outcomes and expectations for mission and offering the idea of a 'complex good' being the outcome of missional pastoral care.

Chapter 5 addresses the theological underpinning of missional pastoral care and the ways differs from the inherited 'working theologies' that mission practitioners can carry into their mission. In their practice, team and community members drew on different biblical and theological resources to support their new approach to their mission. These include reaffirming *missio Dei* as God's way of relating to the world, that all people are made in the image of God, and *shalom* as the incoming peaceable kingdom of God.

Missional pastoral care arises from within the charismatic evangelicalism of the Eden Network, and so Chapter 6 considers the bigger questions and implications of this work for evangelicalism as a tradition. Being aware of our theological tradition helps us overcome any potential blind spots and be more attuned to all that God might be doing in the world. By engaging the experiences of missional practitioners and urban community members with evangelical theology, we can see the ways that God may be drawing evangelicalism forward in its thinking and practice. God is most often found at the margins, and in these stories God's grace and presence are profoundly evident.

Finally, Chapter 7 engages the learnings of missional pastoral care with popular models of mission, such as personal witnessing, exploring-Christianity courses and social action projects. I offer starting points for those wanting to reflect on these themes further and experiment with missional pastoral care in their own contexts. In addition to an Appendix unpacking my practical theological research methodology, I have included a full Bibliography and Further-Reading list. My hope for this book is that it provides a different perspective on mission, which can enable you to see things otherwise obscured and to try new approaches, leading to ever richer participation in God's mission.

We begin our exploration of missional pastoral care with the connection between the two: why put 'missional' with 'pastoral care'? This starts with the desire to see lives changed, and what we might learn about that process from models of pastoral care.

Notes

1 Having moved in, Eden teams remain in their communities indefinitely, engaging with local people in a variety of ways. This often includes running programmed activity, such as youth clubs or work with younger children; it also involves being a proactive neighbour and prioritizing local amenities and services. This may lead to other forms of participation, such as residents, and tenants' groups or governorships for local schools. For more information on the Eden Network, see www.message.org.uk/eden.

2 The language used about people who experience poverty is extremely important. Labelling people as 'the poor' or 'deprived' ignores the full breadth of their personhood, reducing them simply to a socioeconomic demographic. I am grateful to the theologian and activist Andrew Grinnell for the phrase 'people struggling against poverty', which I use here. Helpfully, it presents poverty as an unjust situation and those who experience it as exercising their own agency in their struggle against it.

3 There was some ethnic diversity within the Eden Network at the time of my research, and one of my Eden team-member participants was black British, although as a network it was majority white. While the communities my participants lived in were ethnically diverse to varying degrees, all except one were majority white. This would not be the case for the London Eden teams which, unfortunately, I was not able to include in this research.

2

How People Change – Finding Pastoral Care in Mission

When you think about transforming you think about [a] . . . tree, it starts off as just like a little thing and just expands, so maybe it doesn't change much in particular apart from just getting bigger and bigger and bigger and broadening itself. And I think whether that's your mind, whether that's your heart, whether that's your soul, whether that's your relationship with God or something, transformation is just not necessarily, maybe not changing completely, but broadening. (Jack, 16, urban community member)

Most people are looking to effect change – even if this is just change in themselves. I'm writing this in January and last night there was the opportunity to watch four separate TV programmes across three channels, all related to dieting and losing weight – changing is on most people's agenda in some form and it's by no means simple. In ministry and mission we might see our role as change agents – in other words, seeing change in people is the point. This might include seeing people come to faith in Jesus for the first time; people resolving personal challenges such as addiction or fractured relationships; campaigning for the living wage in your city; or contributing to mentoring schemes for young people involved in gangs. The tricky thing about working for change in others is that the outcome is not up to us. It is not within our power to prevent someone from drinking to excess or to make someone find faith. In our more honest moments we might acknowledge that we struggle to make life changes ourselves, let alone influence others. There is a risk in ministry that we paint a simplistic picture of life change; that some models of working for change in others help us to keep a safe distance from the ambiguity of life change, so that we can talk about seeing 'lives transformed' through our mission and ministry while the ongoing stories of the people involved slip off our radar.

The desire to see lives changed is the common thread between mission and pastoral care. The experiences of Christians involved in urban mission demonstrate that a process of meaning-making commonly accepted within pastoral care is also relevant to mission – it is the substance (the nuts and bolts) of life change. This chapter explores the idea that we all have a meaning-system (a way of understanding the world), and that a combination of a challenge to perspective and an affirmation of personhood can enable our meaning-systems to change. This pattern is already established in models of pastoral counselling, but with these elements at the heart of the missional mode of living I observed among my participants, the two fields come together: mission and pastoral care. While pastoral care focuses on remaking meaning in counselling conversations, in missional pastoral care the same process takes place in community life, through actions as well as words and through a wide network of relationships.

Concern for how people change is explored through many different academic and professional disciplines – psychology, organizational studies, human and community development, theology, education, pastoral care, mission studies. From their different perspectives each seeks to understand the processes of human development and how life change can be enabled. Most recently, developments in neuroscience have brought new insights into how our brains establish patterns of habit and belief and how these can also be changed (Siegel, 2011, p. 5).

One question that can divide opinion is 'What is the first priority: changes to thinking or changes to action?' Some schools of thought suggest that tackling our thoughts and ideas – along with the reasons for them – is the best approach and will lead to changes in behaviour. Others advocate making behavioural changes first, leaving the brain to catch up with the body. In theology this debate is often conceptualized as orthodoxy ('right thinking') or orthopraxy ('right action'). Many in mission contexts grapple with the relation between the cognitive (intellectual) assent to Christian doctrine and the living out of a Christlike lifestyle in the messiness of people coming to faith. The popularity of various forms of 'belong, believe, behave'-style models demonstrates this struggle.

The relationship between human thinking and human doing is a complex one, and setting these up as opposites is unhelpful and unnecessary. There is no such thing as action separate from thought (whether conscious or unconscious) – either that of the person acting or that of the onlooker observing the action. Equally, there is no way to divorce our cognitive beliefs from our actions; we are whole people, and while we are often complex and contradictory, a mystery even to ourselves, the challenge of life change is better addressed by starting with that complexity rather than by adopting artificial distinctions.

The link between our doing and our thinking is 'meaning'. We often use the word 'meaning' in an ultimate sense, referring to the ways in which we review our entire lives, our existence; or perhaps just a distinct period of our life: a job, illness or relationship. Finding meaning in this ultimate way brings us comfort and helps us to navigate the events and challenges that life brings and that often seem utterly random. But we also *make* meaning every day; it is a part of being human. 'Meaning' refers to the significance we attribute to something or how we understand an experience or person. It characterizes the relationship between an experience (our doing) and our interpretation of that experience (our thinking): what we conclude that an experience *means*. And one experience might have a different meaning for each person involved; meaning is very personal. Therefore, meaning can help us overcome the dichotomy between doing and thinking by illuminating the relationship between the two; as a result, it is a critical concept in understanding how people change. Insights from pastoral care, psychology and neuroscience have helped me to understand how the life changes described by the participants in my research have occurred: through the re-evaluation and remaking of their personal meaning-systems.

What is a meaning-system?

The idea of a world view is a familiar one. It describes the particular way of seeing the world held by a person or group. 'Meaning-system' is an overlapping concept. A person's meaning-system is their way of understanding events, people and the world as a whole; it is likely to be the result of both inherited thinking and viewpoints developed throughout their life. The term 'world view' implies that the world looks different to different people depending on where you're standing, hence there can be multiple world views. Meaning-systems explain why these differences exist – different people interpret experiences and events in a variety of ways, according to their standpoint and their previous experiences. They therefore come up with different understandings of what happened, and a meaning-system is the uniquely constructed set of meanings that a person holds and uses to navigate their way through life.

Here is an example: I am an enthusiastic home baker and a while ago I decided to have a go at baking macarons – you know, those beautiful brightly coloured meringue treats. I found a recipe from a trusted source and set about making pink macarons filled with buttercream and raspberry jam. Unfortunately, far from being perfectly round, pink delights, my macaron biscuits were splodges of purple-grey goo. I didn't bother to fill them with the buttercream and jam. This was disappointing, and as an experience there are different ways in which I could have interpreted it. Perhaps the most obvious option would be to conclude that I can't make macarons; that I am not a skilled baker and I should not bother trying again. But I didn't draw that conclusion, and after some macaron-based research, I blamed the food colouring. I had used liquid food colouring and, at the time, it had felt like a lot of extra liquid going into the mixture. As I now know, gel colouring is recommended for macarons for exactly that reason – it creates intense colour with very little liquid. The reason for my rather more optimistic deduction was my baking history. Based on my experience so far, it seemed unlikely that it was my baking skills that were solely to blame for the disastrous macarons. So as a result of my previous experiences, my meaning-system included a belief in myself as a fairly good baker. In this situation I used that meaning-system to help me understand what went wrong with the macarons. I interpreted the situation in the way I did, based on prior baking success.

Another example: what if you had recently moved to a new neighbourhood in order to be a part of a new Fresh Expression of church there? The area has a reputation for crime and social deprivation and you are coming to reach out with the love of God to the people in that place. Your current perception of the community and your understanding of what it means to do mission informs the way you approach your new neighbours. You might bake cookies for them to say hello when you first move in, or look around to see what you can begin to initiate in the area to improve things. That is a particular meaning-system at work, and when your new neighbours don't seem massively grateful or excited about your contribution you might assume that 'their hearts are hardened'. That is the logical conclusion of your meaning-system. But if your expectation is that God has already been at work in your community and that your new neighbours are made in God's image, then perhaps your first action would be to get to know them, listen to their stories and discern what you might learn about God from them and their community.

We use our meaning-systems to interpret our experiences and these interpretations then become a part of our meaning-systems. So let's consider the idea of a meaning-system in more detail.

Meaning and story

Humans construct their meaning-systems primarily as narratives, or stories. At the most basic level, a story is the 'representation of real or fictional situations in a time sequence' (Ganzevoort,

2011, p. 216), and they usually have some distinct elements, including the setting, plot, characters and tone. The setting of the story refers to the 'givens of the situation in which the story takes place' (Gerkin, 1984, p. 113). These could be specific prior events, beliefs or circumstances that shape the story and create a particular atmosphere. The setting creates some expectations for how events will pan out. Plot refers to what happens in the story, the action. Characters are the seen and unseen figures involved in the story, including the story-tellers themselves. A central part of living as a Christian is coming to naturally recognize and acknowledge God as a character in all of our life's stories, sometimes tangibly real, sometimes painfully silent, but always present. The tone of the story expresses the emotional undercurrent of the narrative – is it optimistic and bright, tense and anxious or monotonous and dull? Some people always tell their life's stories in a minor key, whereas others always have a victory march. Tone is rarely explicit but we are acutely tuned to such emotional dynamics, and how we respond to a story is strongly shaped by our (often unconscious) reaction to its tone.

These components become a story when the 'sequence connects events into patterns of causality, desirability, development and meaning' (Ganzevoort, 2011, p. 216). From childhood we ask 'Why?' Understanding how something has come about, whether it is a good or bad experience, and how it fits into our overall life so far seems to be a part of what it means to be human. We use story to literally 'make sense' of life's experiences, sorting through them, sifting out what seems unimportant and connecting events together in such a way as to enable coherence. Daniel Kahneman, the Nobel prize-winning psychologist and economist, describes this as the 'remembering self'. The 'experiencing self' is our awareness and presence in the moment of an experience, and the 'remembering self' orders and gives meaning to life events as we remember them, so that they emerge as a coherent story able to help us maintain a positive self-image (2011, pp. 386–90).

The world of psychology highlights how important this affirming story is for human well-being. The pastoral theologian Charles

Gerkin notes that an inability to reconcile one's life events into a coherent and affirming story leads to psychological suffering (1984, p. 93; see also Sremac, 2014, pp. 36–43). When our experiences do not match our meaning-systems we find ourselves uncomfortable and destabilized. Kahneman describes the ability of our brains to quickly create workarounds for such discomfort, however implausible they might be. But the significance of coherent, positive life stories for our well-being points towards our meaning-systems as holding the potential for human change.

Our culture is full of stories. Marketing bombards us with visual stories, on bill boards, in magazines, YouTube clips and TV ads – the 'look who you could be if you bought this' story. In politics and campaigning we are told 'this is the problem and this is the solution' stories, or 'we can change the world together' stories. In churches we often tell the 'transformed life' story. Some of these stories are helpful and inspiring; they show us what is possible and invite us in. Given how powerful story is for humanity, then, it is unsurprising that we are moved and attracted to becoming a part of a good story. But some uses of story in our culture (and in our churches) do not respect the vulnerability that comes with our need for positive, coherent stories about ourselves. They can also be used carelessly, or even cynically to manipulate people, commodifying us and our hopes and desires for financial gain or a longing for power – the 'if you do/buy/follow this then life will be awesome' story. Stories are powerful because they are the primary way in which we come to understand the world and our place within it. Your meaning-system is a story about the world, about you and your family, your skills and abilities, God, other people, and how the world could – and should – be. In order to change your life, it is necessary to engage with your meaning-system – your life's story.

Changing the story

Life change requires a change in meaning-system, a process that includes words and actions, challenges to thinking alongside support and care from others. Margaret, Jess and Adam offered very different stories of change but each contained these common elements.

Rediscovering faith – Margaret's story

Margaret is a single mum in her forties from Yorkshire. One significant aspect of the story she shared with me when I interviewed her was her recent rediscovery of faith. Margaret had been raised Catholic but, due to a painful bereavement some years before, had 'turned my back on my faith and everything else'. In the years prior to our interview Margaret had been facing some challenges with antisocial behaviour on her estate. She met members of the Eden team and local church at the school gate and described a feeling that 'there was something very unique' about them. A community meal followed and Margaret and her family began to experience welcome and acceptance, totally at odds with the antisocial behaviour that was causing such fear and isolation. She said, 'I felt accepted here so I didn't feel like . . . I'd got to . . . just be on my guard all the time.' As relationships built gradually and Margaret considered whether she wanted to investigate faith again, one of her new friends gave her a Bible; she described her thoughts about this: 'I'll be honest, it was very precious the minute they gave it to me, but at that stage I thought, "Oh I can't really delve into it just yet . . ."' Team members occasionally recommended specific Bible passages for her to read and Margaret went on to explain:

> I kind of looked back at the texts or whatever they'd sent and I'd start looking through and I'd think, 'Oh my goodness, that was really specific . . . that would have helped me so much that day . . .' It's made me see God in exactly the same light but just a little bit brighter.

Over time Margaret has found that her faith has become a resource for facing her own challenges and also offering support to others. She said: 'It just made me feel that I could say to them, you know, well yes I am a Christian and if ever you do want to come for a small burst of prayer or anything else feel free to knock on.'

Managing anger – Jess's story

Jess was 16 when I interviewed her and she lives in Yorkshire; her experiences of overwhelming anger had lasted for a number of years while her mum suffered from cancer. She reflected on anger as a 'bad' way to deal with her mum's illness; it further damaged their relationship and caused Jess and her family a lot of pain. When they moved to the area, Jess's mum started going to church and Jess met members of the Eden team, who involved her in a youth band. She described the way that church impacted her mum:

> It was something new really 'cos she used to go as a child but then obviously with her working and stuff she didn't have time to do stuff like that, but church did calm her down as well, she like, she just seen something different and it helped her a lot . . .

Jess's own relationships with Eden team members grew and she found that:

> . . . I could talk to [team member] whenever I wanted, if I got upset she would talk to me, and it's like I wouldn't, I actually would have no clue what I would be doing right now if it weren't for those two – they've just done so much.

Jess's relationship with her mum is much better now and she's 'got her anger completely settled down'.

Getting to know people – Adam's story

Adam is a team member in his thirties from Greater Manchester; he is married with one son. He described the way that getting to know people in his community has taken him beyond their reputations:

> . . . the guy at the end of our road, he's known to be the hardest guy on our street that people are scared of and his wife . . . kids are just petrified of them, but being intentional and getting to know that family you actually realize they are just reputations . . . it's about getting underneath the skin of the person, finding out who they actually are.

And:

> . . . yeah, last night one of the kids decided to get the fire extinguisher and set it off, you know, like kids do and he came up to me and said 'do you think I'm a really bad kid now, do you think I am really bad?' an' I said 'no, mate, I don't because I know you're not a bad lad, you just made some wrong decisions sometimes' and it's because as a team we spend time getting to know these kids that we can say things like [that] . . . for him to hear that is crazy – you could see his face light up . . . but I can only do that because I know him.

Adam's perception of the people in his community has changed dramatically during his time there, leading to changes in how he sees himself and his ministry as part of an Eden team. He said:

> God really just led me down this kind of journey, you know, [God saying:] 'I'm with this person in exactly the same way that I love you . . . exactly the same way as I love Moses, the same way as I love Noah', you know, and it's like, kind of gets you in the heart a little bit and you think flip, that's crazy and it's our job to communicate that love to them as well . . .

These three stories are just brief insights into the kinds of change processes that my participants described. As I listened to these stories, and many others, I asked myself: What is actually bringing about change here? What are the processes and mechanics of life change and what promotes or hinders it? So let's look at what it is that enabled the changes described by Margaret, Jess and Adam.

Enabling change through hermeneutical play

Running through each of these stories – the stories of everyone I interviewed and those of many people I have talked to since doing this research – is a process that Gerkin refers to as 'hermeneutical play': challenging a person's meaning-system and helping them to experiment with changing the meanings they use to interpret the world around them. You may be more familiar with the word 'hermeneutics' in relation to biblical exposition, but it simply means the art of interpretation. Philosophers such as Hans-Georg Gadamer see hermeneutics as the way we bridge the gap between a text and our own meaning-systems, in order to achieve understanding (Linge, 1976, p. xii). He suggests that hermeneutics involves a creative, generative act between the text and the 'pre-understanding' that a reader brings to it. Rather than just aiming to hear what the author intended in writing, Gadamer argues that reading involves an interplay between the author's intention, the text itself and the reader's meaning-system; this leads to what Gadamer calls a 'fusion of horizons' in which something new, 'understanding', is created (Linge, 1976, pp. xvi–xxviii).

Charles Gerkin adopted Gadamer's hermeneutical theory as a starting point for his model of pastoral counselling. His aim is to enable life change, and in order to do this he recognizes the importance of engaging with the meaning-system of the person seeking help. Gerkin describes the way that – just as one might after a superficial reading of the Bible use 'proof-texts' to make a theological or moral point – in pastoral counselling a superficial listening to what an individual says about themselves and their situation can lead to 'proof-texting'. This means that we think we understand that person (or indeed the Bible!) but in fact we are not taking into account the whole picture, either of the person we are listening to or of our own pre-judgements that we bring to the conversation, and therefore our understanding is limited, even skewed. Gerkin advocates a much deeper engagement with a person, aiming to create a 'fusion of horizons' in which the counsellor comes to really understand the meaning-system of the care-seeker and they can together develop a rich understanding of each other's perspectives and a shared language with which to talk about life experiences (1984, pp. 38–9).

When this fusion of horizons is achieved, a counsellor can talk clearly and with empathy about the care-seeker's situation. This opens up the possibility for discussion of their meaning-system itself, and their particular interpretations of significant life events or relationships. The counsellor may ask provocative questions that lead the care-seeker to question their previous interpretation of a situation, or may offer an alternative way to interpret the life circumstances the care-seeker is facing. Gerkin calls this 'hermeneutical play' – an interactive process in which a person's meaning-system (their way of interpreting the world) is brought to conscious awareness, questioned, and alternative meanings or interpretations of life events, relationships or realities can be experimented with in a safe space (1984, p. 153). He understands this as the core of the pastoral counselling task, through which care-seekers can be helped to change their meaning-systems, finding new ways to understand and navigate the challenges they face.

Describing this process as hermeneutical *play* tells us something important about it. Professor of psychiatry Kay Redfield Jamison understands play as an 'experimental business' that 'is about learning how to learn' and which 'promotes flexibility in . . . thinking and behaviour' (2004, pp. 51–62). Play is a necessity in early life to enable us to develop exploratory skills. That this should be pleasurable and light-hearted is a vital part of the process – it is practising, experimenting and trying out new behaviours to see how they fit, with no requirement for success or permanence. Gerkin sees this lightness and exploration as uniquely enabling people to grapple with their inherited and constructed meaning-systems and also as a space in which the Holy Spirit can be at work; he says: 'The Spirit is always active in the gap between humanly constructed reality and the new reality God is bringing about' (1984, p. 154).

This playful process of reinterpretation that Gerkin sees happening in counselling conversations actually occurs in the daily lives of the people I interviewed. Missional pastoral care as a way of life brings the meaning-systems of those involved to their awareness, and enables a gentle playfulness, over time, leading to exploring new possibilities for understanding the world. So with this in mind, let's return to the stories of Margaret, Jess and Adam. How do we see hermeneutical play taking place in their experiences, and what is it that actually enables the changes they described? I think there are two distinct dynamics at play in each of these stories, which occurred consistently within my data: a challenge to perspective and an affirmation of personhood. When these two factors are present, then a space is opened up in which the creativity of hermeneutical play can take place.

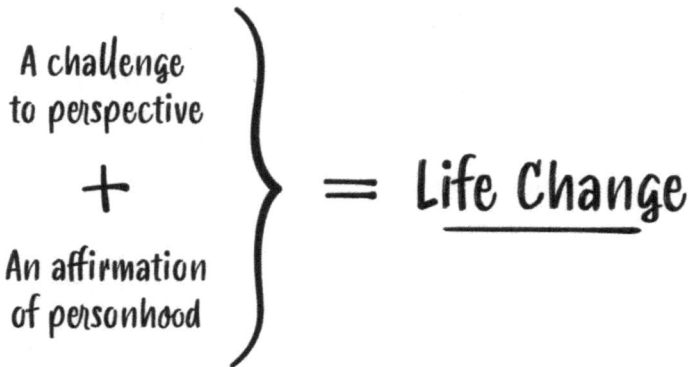

A challenge
to perspective

+

An affirmation
of personhood

$\Big\}$ = Life Change

A challenge to perspective

Each story includes the individual coming to believe that life could be lived differently; that their experience to date is not all that there is and not the only option for living in their situation. For Jess, her fragile relationship with her mum and her uncontrollable emotions began to look strange in contrast to the peace and warmth she experienced with other adults around her. She also articulates the way that going to church impacted her mum – that in church she had 'seen something different' that 'helped her a lot'. Adam discovered the truth of people in his community by getting to know them over time rather than being influenced by their reputations; this led him to realize afresh the universality of God's love. I describe this as a challenge to perspective.

The challenge to perspective comes about in these stories in a wide variety of ways. It is both spoken and observed, incidental and intentional, received and practised, often a combination of all of these. Community member Margaret had responded to her experiences of violence and intimidation by staying at home and keeping her children inside for much of the time, even keeping the curtains closed around the house. She described the way a team member shared his faith as an alternative and challenging narrative:

> I bumped into [him] and he just said, you know, 'You shouldn't be just behind closed doors, that's not how God wanted us to live our lives' . . . and I thought well, you know, I think you're right, and I'm passing that down to my children that it's OK to live in a cave and that's not how you live . . .

Such an explicit verbal challenge occurred as part of an extended process of building relationships: bumping into another team member in the street occasionally, and observing the culture of the church café as inclusive and accepting, a stark contrast to the rejection she had experienced elsewhere.

Many writers, in a variety of fields, have discussed the need for challenges to existing perspectives in order to enable a change in meaning-system. Famously, the scientist Thomas Kuhn writes about the shared 'paradigms' in scientific research that explain how the world works, and the necessity of 'anomalies' that increasingly demonstrate the weaknesses of an existing paradigm in order for a new one to be adopted (1996, pp. 77–8). From the perspective of psychology of religion, Raymond Paloutzian writes about 'spiritual transformations' as changes in meaning-systems, which 'occur because people are confronted with discrepancies in life that require them to construct a new meaning-system because the old one no longer works' (2005, p. 334). In much of this work on meaning-system change, the perception is of a 'crisis', a negative experience that is resolved by the change in thinking. Missional pastoral care demonstrates that while this may be true in some instances, the challenge to perspective can also come more positively, in the form of a surprise or contrast – such as those experienced by Jess, Margaret and Adam above.

For Gerkin, pastoral counselling involves holding up the Christian narrative alongside the narrative of the individual seeking help, just as the team member did for Margaret above. The Christian narrative provides a contrasting meaning-system, offering that challenge to perspective and opening up the possibility of a different interpretation of reality. Gerkin also gives this an eschatological twist: that by offering an alternative story we invite people into the incoming kingdom of God in their own life and in the wider community and world (1986, pp. 54–5). By offering this challenge to perspective, Gerkin maintains that the care-seeker can be helped to live into their eschatological self, the self as God sees it, sustained by hope and the work of the Spirit (1984, p. 69).

An affirmation of personhood

The second factor in these stories (and central to my understanding of mission as a result of this research) is the individual feeling accepted and valued for who they are, as they are, and being active participants in the process of their change. This combination of acceptance and agency can be described as an affirmation of 'personhood'.

This was a surprising finding for me in the research. I expected from my own observations and experiences that the differences between mission practitioners and the people they came to live alongside would be significant in catalysing life change, but as I listened to my participants they also talked about staying the same. For example, Jess talked about the change she went through in dealing with her anger. She said 'my personality's completely changed', but later in the interview she described herself as: 'I've always been happy, but then there's times when I'm bad, when I'm like really unhappy but the happiness is always there.' Sixteen-year-old Jack offered a beautiful description of transformation, which I used to open this chapter:

> When you think about transforming you think about [a] . . . tree, it starts off as just like a little thing and just expands, so maybe it doesn't change much in particular apart from just getting bigger and bigger and bigger and broadening itself. And I think whether that's your mind, whether that's your heart, whether that's your soul, whether that's your relationship with God or something, transformation is just not necessarily, maybe not changing completely but broadening.

He went on to illustrate this process as he's seen it in his friend:

> . . . he's a friend of mine but really he wasn't very good, but he didn't change like, he, he just broadened. He didn't change particularly as a person, I saw him grow but maybe not properly change, I think he stayed him which made [him] quite easy to talk to, and as he grew in faith, which means as he grew and broadened but stayed him.

The odd tension between radical life change and staying the same illustrates the importance of a coherent life narrative for our well-being. My participants acknowledged huge changes in their meaning-systems but also asserted that they were 'still them'. This led me to reflect on what being 'still them' might mean: what is a self?

At the core of being human is personhood: the worth, wonder and reality of your existence. Personhood is a more fundamental category than identity, which might refer to the nature or content of a person – for example, kind, good at sports or greedy. Identity is dynamic, and challenges with issues such as mental health may mean that 'who I am' feels like a shifting concept. Jess's words illustrate this sense of her happy nature being muddied by the pain she was experiencing due to her mum's illness. For me, her description of the 'happiness' that is 'always there' reaches beyond personality or identity to something more fundamental and universal: personhood, which refers to the fact and gift of our existence and humanity, an inherent goodness not dependent on identity or action. Agency is the exercising of personhood; simply by our existence the world is changed. When we take action, make choices or even remain passive, circumstances and relationships are altered. This is the consequence of our personhood; we cannot help but make a difference, however small, in the world.

The theologian Anthony Reddie calls this 'subjectivity' and finds affirmation for human personhood within the doctrine of *imago Dei*: humanity made in the image of God, to which we will return in a later chapter. He writes: 'God's freedom to act and to be an infinite, transcendent being is bestowed upon humanity, who also possess these very same qualities of self-definition, transcendence, and agency . . . Subjectivity is the ability to create meaning and be a constructive being in creating and remaking one's world' (2018, p. 8).

Affirming the personhood of others happens through the words and actions of those around them and by the way in which those around them receive their agency and action. Jess was offered acceptance by team members as they supported and listened to her in the midst of her challenges. Adam's story indicates the acceptance he received from local people. As he got to know them they also in turn came to know and care for him. The concept of personhood will keep cropping up throughout these chapters. Theology that affirms the personhood of every human being, and mission models that respect it and give space for people to exercise their agency are, I believe, essential for human flourishing. But theological, sociological and cultural factors often mean that we believe and act in ways that do not respect personhood and do not receive the gift of every human being. This has to change if our mission is to make a contribution to God's incoming *shalom*.

The process of hermeneutical play that enables a change in meaning-system occurs when both of these elements, a challenge to perspective and an affirmation of personhood, are present. If we only receive a challenge to perspective without an affirmation of our fundamental goodness and worth then we may not feel safe enough to engage with new ideas. The challenge is received negatively and is too much to bear so we protect ourselves and resist change. Most likely, our response is to shut down, reject the new and remain possibly entrenched in our views. If, on the other hand, we receive an affirmation of our personhood without any challenge to perspective, then there is no opportunity to consider ways that the world might be different. We are stuck with only our experiences of life so far, and therefore are unable to take steps to change patterns in our lives that may be destructive but that genuinely appear to us to be the only plausible option.

When both of these factors come together we feel safe enough to entertain new ideas and ways of being without needing to protect ourselves. We can be open to the new while remaining authentically ourselves, and can begin to play: experimenting with new ways of thinking and being in the world and in our relationships. In time, as our experiments offer us new experiences and ideas, adding evidence to the initial challenge to our perspective, our meaning-systems change and we adopt different ways of seeing ourselves, other people, our communities, God and the world around us.

'Parabolic' relationships – hermeneutical play in daily life

The theologian John Dominic Crossan describes 'parable' as a form of language that plays the role of subverting accepted meanings in constructed worlds (1988, p. 42; Gerkin, 1984,

p. 161). The parable of the Good Samaritan that is in Luke 10 offers an example. In the story Jesus sets a scene, familiar to his listeners, of travel, a tragic crime and a need for help; thus far he confirms the world view (and meaning-systems) of his listeners. But in an unforeseen twist, Jesus makes the Samaritan the hero of the story. The one who was despised, whom the beaten man would have least wanted to touch him or help him, he is the one who offers an example to Jesus' Jewish audience of neighbourliness that pleases God. While many of Jesus' stories can seem alien to Western, twenty-first-century, urban ears, for his audience – near-Middle Eastern, first-century, semi-rural communities – they were both reassuringly familiar and oddly disconcerting. Jesus made the familiar strange, painting pictures of their world made different, subverted by a God who didn't play along with their meaning-systems but who offered a radically new interpretation of reality: the kingdom of God.

So a parable is a subversive story, one that opens up the possibility of new ways of seeing the world. Arguably Jesus is himself like a parable in that he embodied that new way, the kingdom of God, and was certainly not the kind of messiah that the people expected or hoped for. In fact, Crossan notes that Jesus was known among the early Church as the 'Parable of God' (1992, p. viii). We might do well to ask ourselves how disturbing or subversive we find Jesus; if the answer is 'not very', then maybe we're not receiving his profound challenge to our own contemporary meaning-systems!

Charles Gerkin uses this idea of a parable as a subversive person or story and describes the relationship between counsellor and care-seeker in pastoral care as 'parabolic' – that is, having the same subversive character as a parable (sorry, nothing to do with geometry for those of you whose minds went there!).

The idea of a relationship that is like a parable seems resonant with the experiences of team and community members. In missional pastoral care, networks of interlinked relationships are formed that shift and change, ebb and flow over time but have this subversive, parabolic character to them. Both mission practitioners and urban community members experience a degree of subversion of life narratives in getting to know one another. This happens as they challenge one another's perspectives and as they offer a loving affirmation of one another's personhood. The result is that both parties revise their meaning-systems to acknowledge and account for the other's experience and the shared experience built through the relationship. It is the same process as Charles Gerkin identifies in pastoral counselling, but it is happening in a much wider context: in a community, over a greater period of time, and across a network of relationships and different kinds of encounters and activities. Let me demonstrate.

Parabolic relationships in action

Life-giving openness – Kevin's story

Kevin had known team members in his community for three years when I interviewed him, but had had a ten-year history of being with other Christians living locally who ran a community project. Kevin was 23 and had spent part of his childhood in care, having experienced abuse and neglect. When he described his interactions with team members he often described them as 'open', 'open to him', and the way that they 'opened' him up. Kevin got to know one family in particular:

> [team member] invited me for tea once . . . he just, he got a new house . . . and he was like keeping me occupied, he said do you want to come and give me a hand, fixing this . . . so I said yeah, had tea with 'em, all that kind of stuff . . .

During the same time frame Kevin started volunteering at the local project; he said:

> . . . while I were doing the voluntary work it give me more confidence in meself, like, you know meeting different people in there, people like me but, you know, getting to know them more better because I was part of the team in

there . . . I felt like more confidence was, you know, coming out of me and stuff like that.

Kevin described his history of self-harm, and explained that when he was very low it felt like a release. Later in our conversation he described his venturing into faith in a similar way: 'Going to church . . . it made me feel better, I felt like I could release things that I've never been able to release before'. The combination of team members and the Christians already active in their community provided a varied network for Kevin to connect with in more formal ways such as volunteering, and informally through church and friendships. The kind of release and openness he observed and experienced as he began to get to know people, pray and explore church subverted his past experiences of being unable to release pain and emotion except through self-harm. He described his relationship with one team member:

> . . .we just have a laugh, dead open, like me when I was like, when I was about 18 I was like, out of 100 per cent I was like 40, 45 per cent, you know in confidence and stuff like that but now I reckon I'm like a good . . . 75, 80 per cent . . .

Discipleship as community – David's story

When I interviewed community member David he was 20 and had known the Eden team in his community for 12 years. His first encounter with the team was in itself a surprise. He and his friends had broken into the garden of a supposedly derelict house but found themselves confronted by a team member who had recently moved in. David described: 'Rather than doing what you'd expect someone to do and be really angry she was really calm and really happy and, just supportive.' That was the beginning of a whole network of relationships that David later described as 'my second family'. He talked about losing touch with the team for a few years as he went to secondary school, but he ended up reconnecting when a friend invited him to church:

I was talk[ing] to a friend, just about what my plans were for the weekend and he was telling me what he was doing and he said that on Sunday he was going to go to church and I was like you're going to church, didn't think you went to church, you're not religious are you? He was like, no I'm not religious but there's a bunch of people that I know and they're all really friendly and stuff and we go and we all have a meal and we all chat with each other, and he invited me along and I was like OK I'll go just to see what it's about . . .

. . . I just remember looking round, and I saw all these people that I used to know, that lived in the estate . . . and it didn't take me long at all to get really involved and really connected with them,'cos they were all welcoming and supportive, and they didn't really care where you came from, your background and stuff like that.

David eventually came to call himself a Christian and his experiences of befriending the team have profoundly informed his faith. He talked about Eden as being 'on a micro scale . . . where you're actually able to talk to them regular . . .' Later in his interview I asked David what he understood by the word 'discipleship', and he replied 'You think of discipleship being like, having followers, but it's not, it's community.'

People very different from me – Hannah's story

Hannah is an Eden team member and she offers a different perspective on the way that relationships have subverted her previous assumptions. She talked about her own nervousness about moving to a council estate that had a bad reputation, but in joining the team she became part of 'living in a church community which is amazing and I really like doing that because you're just round the corner from everybody and the youth come and knock on the door and that's cool too'. She continued: 'I think I am learning to be a bit more laid back. I'm not sure whether that's the area or whether it's church as well . . . learning to open your door a bit more to people.'

As Hannah became a part of this community and opened herself up to relationships, she has recognized the change this has brought about for her:

> . . . just learning more about people, which again sounds fairly bizarre for [me] because [in my job] I see people all the time but actually I don't work with people that are very different to me all the time and here it is like that and it is really challenging but really good, so I think we have grown a lot in our understanding of where people are coming from.

Hannah was aware that she had also subverted the assumptions of the young people she befriended simply by staying in her community long term. She said:

> . . . it shows itself in relationship because they begin to trust you and they are not constantly asking you 'Are you leaving?' They kind of assume you are going to be around which is good and the way it should be really . . . they know you are going to be there at the end of the phone if they need you and stuff.

In each of these stories we see elements of meaning-systems being challenged and changed over time and through ongoing community relationships. For Kevin, the openness and friendship he received challenged the negative self-image that he carried as a result of childhood trauma. David found a different kind of family in the team who weren't religious in the way he expected and who opened up new ways of thinking about God and Christian faith. Team member Hannah became aware of the way that her life could be completely orientated around 'people like her' and she found that this changed as she joined an Eden team, bringing a whole new perspective on the world as well as changes in her lifestyle.

In each case, building relationships with people who are in some way 'different', but who offer acceptance and support alongside their difference, has been a catalyst for changes in thinking and in lifestyle. In the course of these relationships a gentle, and sometimes less gentle, subversion has taken place. Whether this has been intentional, such as talking about the way they see the world with others, or whether it is brought about simply by existing and being themselves around one another, the contrast has been evident and has invited some kind of response. Relationships that have this subversive, parabolic quality to them play a central role in the process of deconstruction, experimentation and reconstruction of our personal meaning-systems that is hermeneutical play; and it is this hermeneutical play that enables life change.

What does this model of life change mean for mission?

Considering mission activity in the light of this process of community-based hermeneutical play, and the challenge to perspective and affirmation of personhood as the core conditions that enable it, can be extremely helpful. Some forms of mission, such as the traditional stereotype of 'hellfire preaching', can focus solely on bringing a challenge to perspective, and then wonder why it is not yielding the fruit that is hoped for as people hunker down and protect themselves from such an overwhelmingly negative assessment of their life. Equally, some kinds of mission activity can focus solely on the affirmation of personhood, with Christians so self-conscious of their difference that they seek to eliminate it altogether. This creates two issues: first, mission practitioners risk not being their authentic selves in their communities, so mission becomes exhausting and ultimately unsustainable; and second, as it simply joins people in their meaning-systems without offering any contrast to them, it again fails to yield the hoped-for life change in those they encounter. Mission models are inevitably shaped by our theology of mission and, as we shall see as we unpack missional pastoral care in more depth, theology can sometimes prove unhelpful as we seek to undertake mission that affirms personhood and challenges perspective.

The process of hermeneutical play occasioned by a challenge to perspective and the affirmation of personhood is not unique to this research. In fact, if you reflect on times in your own life when you have experienced significant change, you may be able to trace the same dynamics at play. How did you feel safe enough or confident enough to reconsider your beliefs/behaviour? What was it that first opened your eyes to a different way of seeing the world? Was it a conversation or a series of events over time? How have the significant people in your life been parabolic to you? Despite this being the way that life change happens, we rarely talk about it in these terms and, as a result, our attempts at enabling life change in others can be misguided and even unhelpful.

By acknowledging and foregrounding this process we put pastoral care at the centre of mission. The presence of Charles Gerkin's model of pastoral care – hermeneutical play – in the stories of Eden team members and urban community members led me to think of this ministry as a form of pastoral care. But the clearly stated intention of the Eden Network and team members is mission. This research shows that pastoral care is not a separate activity only undertaken within churches and among Christians, but that it is missional as well. 'Missional pastoral care' is hermeneutical play within a whole community orientated towards life change. In the next chapter we'll see what this looks like in practice for team members and community members themselves.

3

Missional Pastoral Care in Practice

Missional pastoral care is an intentional way of life shaped by seven elements: difference, locality, availability, practicality, long-term commitment, consistency and love. It enacts the mission of God in three ways: by holistically sharing our lives [for the common good] with those we once saw as 'other'; by talking about our life stories, including faith stories; and by engaging in mutual hermeneutical play, a process of meaning-making that leads to life change for all involved.

This definition begins to describe the kinds of practices and experiences my participants shared with me. Missional pastoral care includes an articulation of faith – avoiding an unhelpful separation between living Christianly and talking about what you believe. At its core is engagement in mutual hermeneutical play, allowing your meaning-system to be challenged by those you meet just as you might challenge theirs. The seven elements of missional pastoral care create a sphere in which relationships of hermeneutical play can occur.

You will notice that living locally, usually involving relocation, is the foundation of missional pastoral care. The Eden Network has a defined model for its mission teams that begins with relocation, and this is outlined in the Network's Five Cornerstones and Five Distinctives.[1] Missional pastoral care is not the model proposed by the Eden Network, but Eden's commitment to relocation and living long term among a community has provided the starting point for missional pastoral care to develop. Eden's innovation and willingness to venture into the unknown, confident that God was with its members, has led to missional pastoral care as an emerging missional approach. While it retains some features in common with the Eden model, missional pastoral care develops and extends these in practice and in the spiritual practices and theological convictions that sustain it. This chapter illustrates the elements of missional pastoral care using the experiences of team and community members, and along the way reflects theologically on some of the practical and ethical challenges they raise, especially questions of power and mutuality.

Living missional pastoral care

Community member Suzy is 19 and from Manchester; she first met the team in her area when she was nine years old. Here she summarizes the relationships she developed with team members and their significance for her and her dad:

I think more having the support of people saying 'Look you can do it, if you put your mind to it', 'cos at home my dad was, well, a lot of the time he was in the pub so I didn't have the support at home, so I end up getting it from the Eden team . . .

. . . I used to spend quite a lot of time with Lynn, I think I used to spend four or five days with Lynn after work, that's just going round, going on the computer and just chilling out, having something to eat . . . Lynn was like my mum, figure 'cos I never had my mum . . . me and Lynn used to go for days out, to the shops or just chilling out in the garden . . . It was mainly chilling and talking about how my life's changing and how I was feeling at the time and how the bullying was affecting me and . . . my schoolwork . . . Lynn helped me a lot with my schoolwork to keep me on track outside of school, so amazing.

. . . Lynn and Julie eventually started involving my dad in things, so getting me and my dad to do things as parent and daughter which we hadn't done in a long time. Lynn helping my dad out with how to keep the housework on top and stuff like that, inviting him over for food . . . so I had the support and then I had my dad's support it's like 'I want to know God now'.

Suzy describes frequent, varied and meaningful encounters with team members. She sees Lynn and Julie as family, even parental figures, and spends regular time with them relaxing and having fun. They also shared in more purposeful activity such as schoolwork, listening to Suzy as she processed her experiences of being bullied, or offering practical support with household tasks for both Suzy and her dad.

Difference, locality, availability, practicality, long-term commitment, consistency and love are evident in Suzy's story and in those of all of my participants, offering a pattern for a missional way of living which, this research shows, can enable life change through challenging personal meaning-systems and reframing them. So let's look at each in detail and build up a picture of this way of life.

Difference

For team and community members getting to know one another, one of the first things they recognized was the differences between them. This may relate to a whole range of factors, from personal preferences to inherited identities. Simply choosing to live locally was in itself a stark contrast, as community member David remembers:

> . . . it was really good just to have someone right within the streets we were living in who actually cared about everyone there 'cos a lot of the time . . . people [were] so hostile towards the idea of gangs and robbers and crime in the area . . .

In one sense this might seem obvious, and some differences – such as accent – were immediately apparent. But as relationships developed, the differences between team members and community members shaped them in some important ways. Community member Clare, in her mid-thirties and from Greater Manchester, describes her first experience of going to church along with the team:

> I think it was the people who went there as well, it wasn't like the people you'd normally meet, they thought a lot of theirselves, they thought a lot of their health, you know of each other, things like that . . .

She continued:

> . . . there's some . . . live here, there's a lot of drugs . . . and you have to get yourself away from it, d'y'know what I mean, but I think going to church helped me do that, to think this is not all of – you don't have to be like this to be cool, to be good.
> . . . because they live here, they live in the same place you live so you can all relate I suppose. 'Cos if they say something to you, you can't [say] 'Oh well, I can't do that 'cos I live on [this estate]' [because they] live on [the estate] as well. . .

In getting to know the team, Clare discovered a group of people who lived in the same location but by a different set of values. This caused her to reflect on her own life and the community she inhabited, introducing the possibility of making different choices. As we saw in Chapter 2, difference creates awareness of alternative ways of being – it provides the challenge to perspective that is essential for enabling life change.

But difference is also a problematic feature of missional pastoral care. Many people seeking to do incarnational mission struggle with the differences between them and their community, seeing it as a hindrance rather than a help in their ministries. This uncertainty is rooted in issues of power and how we define incarnation, which I will explore later in this chapter. For now, suffice to say that missional pastoral care involves building significant relationships with people who are different from you, resisting the desire to mask or dissolve difference but instead allowing these differences to become a part of the dynamic of the relationship.

Local

As Clare and David describe above, these 'different' people moved in around the corner. Missional pastoral care involves being in the same place as those you are building relationships with. This is part of the gift of the Eden Network model: team members focus on a relatively small and defined area and 'live local' (Wilson, 2012, p. 114), prioritizing time in the community and using local facilities alongside other residents. In part this is a response to the significance of local geography in the communities themselves and, for my participants, it represented empathy with the people there, insight and proactive involvement. In missional pastoral care the isolation and fragmentation of marginalized communities is addressed as team members move beyond simply living there to become 'insiders', invested in the same issues and concerns and able to understand the reality of the lives of those around them. It is this that

James, a single team member in his twenties from Greater Manchester, articulates:

> For me it's all about changing a lifestyle, it's not just like 'Oh, you know, we're youth workers, we come on to the estate nine-to-five then go back to our nice houses', you know it's very much become part of the community, live side by side, you struggle with your neighbours in what they're struggling with . . .

This commitment did not go unnoticed, as David commented:

> They can see around 'em like what's going on and they became part of the community rather than just being an outsider who's trying to come in and improve it just to make themselves look good, they were part of the community and said let's be the change of the community ourselves.

Missional pastoral care begins with proximity, sharing space, but goes on to become solidarity. It is about discerning the patterns of life in your community and choosing to make them your own. Moving beyond exclusivity and constructed communities of 'people like us', locality attends to the 'accidental neighbours' – not just the 'chosen ones' – and means that we become a 'local'. As team member Louise said: '. . . it's the longest amount of time I have ever lived in one place which is just really cool, [it] really feels like my home.' In doing so, it leads to participation in creating the sense of place, shared identity and belonging that Baker argues is needed in order to address the issues facing marginalized communities (2009, pp. 126–7).

Available

Living locally enables availability as a further element of missional pastoral care, resonating with the commitment to incarnational presence within urban theology (Davey, 2001, pp. 93–4;

Graham and Lowe, 2009, p. xv). Team member Dan describes his approach to availability:

> . . . it's took up quite a bit of my time . . . not so much now 'cos I live in a flat and it's just changed a bit but when I first moved in there was loads of kids knocking on . . . it means that a lot of time and effort has gone into that 'cos you just have to be, like, open to 'em whenever and even if they come round and start knocking on your door and peeing on your doorstep and juggling with firelighters while they're lit you know . . . it['s] just a very simple thing, I've spent a lot of time doing it, so other people would've done other things but I just did that . . . you decide what you want to invest in don't you, your priorities in your life, and that was one of them . . .

In Dan's beautiful and real commitment to availability he demonstrates both intention and flexibility. He has chosen being available over other possible ways to live, which resonates with team member Hannah's description of the way that being available challenged some of her habits: '. . . it's helping me to come out of my schedule a little bit more and find time, intentionally spend time with people or to be deliberately a bit more hanging around rather than appointment to appointment.' The impact of availability is seen in the development of trusting relationships with others in the community. As Jack put it:

> The fact that they were living on here it made it a lot easier to confide in the Eden team members 'cos you saw them kind of like as just next door, not as someone who was going to take your problems all the way over there.

A combination of locality and availability created safe space for Jack to be open with team members about the challenges he faced.

A commitment to locality and availability also enables shared experiences and regular interaction, creating the opportunity for Gerkin's fusion of horizons and hermeneutical play to take place. Sometimes it occurs as literal play; for example, community member Paul described the way he and his friends behaved when they were young teenagers: '. . . if it was still raining we'd go and cause trouble [so] we'd get to go in his house, so that's what we used to do all the time . . .' Other times it is accidental – for example, Clare, not anticipating the challenge to her meaning-system that would follow, coming to church and discovering 'they weren't like the people you'd normally meet, you know'.

Team member Sally tells the story of a friend on the estate:

> There's a mum of a lad who was about eight or nine when we moved here and his mum is the same age as me . . . and our lives are just worlds apart and yet she was always just so interested in me . . . And there was a couple of things that happened a few years ago that she was quite distraught about and we were able to put her in touch with some people who could offer some counselling . . . and she so appreciated that, like no one would've ever thought that she was worth taking the time to sort something out for . . . the family that she's a part of are quite influential on the estate as well as quite vocal, and actually she's always been sort of a positive advocate for us because she's our neighbour . . .

A fusion of horizons and the creative space that this opens up is developed over time in the ordinariness of being neighbours and friends in a community. Missional pastoral care might include occasions when significant conversations or events brought insight but, as seen above, much of the richness of life does not occur in formal interactions. Care happens over time and through the working out of relationships in daily life.

What about boundaries?

Such availability may well prompt concerns about the personal safety of team or community members and also whether being available in this way is realistic in the long term. These are important issues and have been points of learning for the Eden Network throughout its now 21-year history. Christian models of leadership and ministry can be confused or even conflicted about boundaries, and within mission and leadership circles busy-ness (with its illusion of efficacy) is often prized above self-care. As the theologian Jan Berry notes, some models of ministry emphasize 'unconditional self-giving and availability', making 'talk of boundaries . . . feel like a denial of the Christlike nature of love which is required in pastoral care' (2014, p. 205).

The team members in my research were all from evangelical backgrounds and, as we shall see in Chapter 6, activism is strongly embedded in evangelical identity and theology. Therefore, maintaining a sustainable life balance is sometimes a challenge for Eden teams, who are motivated by a strong sense of calling and evangelical activism. Wilson acknowledges that support for team members in the early years of the Network was inadequate, with some leaving Eden suffering burnout and disillusionment (2012, p. 74). But as the Network matured, helping team members reflect on boundaries and life balance became an important priority.

A driven or unboundaried conception of care is not neutral. It is embedded in understandings of mission or social engagement in which 'we' the Church 'do care' 'to' or 'for' people in order to win them for Jesus. This creates a weight of obligation on the mission practitioner. Missional pastoral care involves a different kind of relationship – mutual, long-term and an end in itself, not simply a means to the end of evangelism. So availability may be described as an intentionally open orientation, rather than a lack of boundaries; it changes over time according to circumstances but maintains a commitment to hospitality and a willingness to engage.

Practical

As all of these stories illustrate, missional pastoral care is fundamentally practical. It may involve programmed diversionary activity such as a youth club or, as in Sally's account of her friendship with a local mum, a more informal relationship built up over time. Community member Jess described joining a youth band as her first association with the team: 'I started going and it were really fun, it were something I could do, something I could, like, go out and just like forget everything what's happened.' Doing things together, choosing to get involved and join in, is a vital component of missional pastoral care. It is part of affirming one another's personhood in that it requires a combination of encouragement and affirmation with agency and initiative. Jess was invited and encouraged to join the band, and in choosing to get involved she found something she enjoyed and where she could use her creative gifts.

Experiences like these show that hermeneutical play happens through actions as well as words. Team member Louise's story offers another example:

> I remember one woman who comes from quite a large family . . . when I met with her, she'd talk a lot and I would listen a lot and I'd be aware that she wasn't good at listening . . . but sometimes I'll be there and they'll be all together . . . they'd all be like talking at one another which made me think when I meet up with her in the week even if she has just 20 minutes or an hour of someone just giving her attention and listening to what she has to say and caring . . . that could be quite a big thing . . .

By spending time listening to her friend, Louise noticed that she was acting in contrast to this woman's experience of family relationships. Louise's perseverance in listening was a deliberate missional action that subverted her friend's meaning-system by enacting an alternative narrative more true to the gospel: that she is worthy of attention.

Community members also described their choices to take certain actions or adopt specific practices as part of the interplay of missional pastoral care relationships. Margaret describes how taking up the practice of Bible reading brought her peace and helped her to choose a way forward for her family: 'I found myself at night putting away my *Take a Break* and me *Bella* and me *Chat* and reading the Bible and I found so much peace with it and I just thought I want to invest in the church . . .'

This action may also be undertaking practices of care for others. As Margaret continues: 'It's widened me as a mum, whereas I thought before it was just my children, I've got enough strength and enough love now for other people's children.' Courage to take on responsibility comes as meaning-systems are reshaped through practical actions. Suzy remembered how she felt when she was asked to help out at youth club:

> . . . they give you responsibilities for doing the tuck shop or clearing up or setting up so we used to help quite a lot . . . It made me realize that people had faith in me to do things. That they can say actually 'Oh look, you are old enough and you can do it' and having the support saying, 'Look, we trust you to do this.'

The practical nature of missional pastoral care means that affirmation of personhood isn't just about words but is also expressed in action. This gives both team and community members the opportunity not only to think of themselves differently as a result of the contrasting experiences of encountering one another, it also begins the process of practising life differently.

Long-term and consistent

Team members frequently encounter the assumption in their community that they aren't staying long, as Adam described:

> . . . when I first moved in 2006 the one question I was asked by almost every person that I met was 'How long are you going to be here for, are you just here for six months and then going?' . . . it wasn't until that six-month period that my relationship with young people changed, they began to trust me a little bit more because I'd been there for eight months, then a year and so on . . . it screams out that you

are here for the long term, that you are not just flitting in and out.

Being willing to enter into a long-term commitment and remain consistent in your presence and neighbourliness in the community communicates respect and value to the people you live alongside. It also allows time for growth in people and in relationships, as Sally's relationship with a local young person illustrates:

> . . . about five years ago now, there was a young lad who had a lot of stuff going on at home . . . he used to regularly take an overdose and then come and knock on our door and collapse on the doorstep . . . so we used to just encourage him to if he felt like he needed to do something like that then come and knock on the door . . . and let's try and talk it out a bit . . . now as an adult we don't see him for months at a time and if there's a drama going on in his life he turns up on the doorstep, he'll sit here for three or four hours, he'll talk it all out, we'll pray with him at the end of it and he'll go and we won't see him again for, you know, another five or six months until the next drama arrives . . . he knows that we're reliable . . . he just never had anybody like that in his life that he could just talk things through with.

Sally and her husband represented stability for that young person, and Hannah agrees that this is also significant in her community: '. . . people do move around and their lives aren't very stable [so] to have people who are there through their teenage years while everything else is chaotic around them is really important.' Rather than looking for neat end-points or a rapid impact, missional pastoral care is about resting in constancy in a community – recognizing that God is at work in the winding paths of hermeneutical play as it takes place over years. This enables strong, mutually significant relationships to be built that lead to the final feature of missional pastoral care: love.

Love – the affirmation of personhood in practice

The stories shared so far illustrate the way of life of missional pastoral care; it involves intentionally investing in relationships with people who are different from you. Living close by means taking opportunities to share your life with people, noticing who you see regularly at the shops, pubs or exercise classes you attend. Making yourself available for these relationships to grow, for these people to become your people, is part of missional pastoral care, and this happens in the mundane practicalities of life as well as in the crises or the dramatic. As one team member commented: '. . . being able to ring up my neighbour and say I think I've left me oven on, can you pop round and check . . .'

Within missional pastoral care, love is what affirmation and respect for personhood looks like in practice. As I described in Chapter 2, maintaining a coherent personal life narrative and a stable sense of self is essential for human well-being. Lasting life change is achieved by integrating changes in our meaning-systems into a pre-existing life narrative, not by scrubbing out our life narrative and starting again (Gerkin, 1984, p. 100). While they do challenge one another's perspectives through their differences, team and community members also accept one another as they are for who they are.

This kind of non-judgemental acceptance led to a number of participants describing their relationships as like 'family'. Jess said:

> . . . you just feel better about yourself and half the time you're like 'I can do that', like they inspire you to do stuff . . . It's like your family, like you can talk to them about anything and they wouldn't judge you, they wouldn't think owt bad, they'd just help yer and it's really good, it's just like your family, that's what you need.

Given time and space, missional pastoral care develops small networks of close, non-judgemental and safe relationships in a local area; these not only benefit those involved, but also contribute to the strengthening of community resilience in the neighbourhood as a whole.

Power and incarnation

The differences of background, faith commitment and the fact of having chosen to relocate as part of a missional initiative create an instant sense that team members and community members are 'other' to one another. While it's clear that this difference can be a positive factor in missional pastoral care, it also undoubtedly creates an imbalance of power in relationships. That this relocation is into communities identified by government data as marginalized adds to this tension; many local people may not have the resources to choose to relocate anywhere, and the very fact of team members choosing where they will live is itself a sign of privilege.[2] In addition, there are important questions about vested interests and power dynamics in ministry among vulnerable people that need to be addressed.

Two features of the Eden Network model of mission help to undermine the unequal distribution of power. First, the majority of team members are not professionals; they are volunteers with their own careers (aside from Eden team leaders, who are usually employed and may have a qualification in youth or community work). Most, apart from a small minority of Eden team leaders, are not ordained or responsible for a congregation of Christians, and team members usually have no official title or qualification for offering pastoral care. Second, on their relocation they become visitors, and community members hold the power of local knowledge. This can be expressed in some quirky ways, as community member Paul tells it:

> . . . years ago, like, another two lads . . . they, like, give 'em all names . . . like a nickname each, so like . . . every time a new one come . . . these two lads give 'em a name and they'd be, like, that's their name now . . . they're happy with it so it makes everybody else feel happy by calling that person that, so then they feel more comfortable around them . . . 'cos everyone says that this is a bad place, so obviously they're not from round here, they're going to think 'Oh, this is a bad

place I'll try to settle in', you know . . . coming from smaller background challenging a bigger background.

It might seem surprising for Paul to describe Eden teams as coming from a 'smaller background' into his 'bigger background' but that is the way he sees it. In his story team members became vulnerable, accepting their new names and becoming a part of their new community.

Despite the non-professional role of the Eden team member and the rebalancing of power caused by relocation, tensions remain within incarnational models of mission. The Eden Network has done a lot of learning and work addressing these concerns over the years (see the Eden Network's own publications, particularly Matt Wilson's *Concrete Faith*, 2012), but subtle ethical and theological questions remain that team members are often instinctively aware of, but may not have fully processed. Missional pastoral care, as I have seen it in the stories of my participants, is a development of the Eden model; it points towards the need to name and dismantle inequalities in relationship that are based in class, poverty and faith commitment, seeking different ways to be alongside others in communities.

Class

It is not always popular to talk about class, but our country is more economically unequal today than it was 50 years ago (Atherton, 2014, pp. 36–7), and the increasing gap between the richest and the poorest in our society falls broadly along class lines. The author Lynsey Hanley writes about her own experiences of growing up on a Birmingham council estate. She says:

> . . . the higher your social status, the more self-confidence tends to be ingrained in you. The further up the social ladder you are, the more external influences are set up to favour you and your kind, to the extent that privilege becomes

invisible and so weightless that – literally – you don't know how lucky you are. At the other end of the social scale, there is an acute sense of how little social trust or esteem is placed in you as an individual, a feeling that is absorbed and then expressed in low self-confidence. (2017, pp. x–xi)

This account demonstrates the implications of class inequality for our emotional well-being and, by extension, our entire lives. Economic, political and social inequality creates communities that are fragmented, in which marginalized groups become trapped, developing a protective self-understanding and a negative reputation among those outside (Baker, 2009, p. 27). As Paul comments:

'Cos where a lot of these are from it's all posh an' all that, innit, and they come here and are all 'Oh [estate name]'. But I don't think it's a bad place but obviously everybody else does, so that's their challenge to change themselves, int it, to get to be liked by everyone here.

Paul's perspective highlights that – on relocating – mission practitioners cross social and economic boundaries and encounter issues of marginalization and deprivation in their new relationships. The middle-class backgrounds of many team members contrast with those in their urban communities who struggle against the constraints of poverty. As Hannah observed: 'People here are from a completely different background, it's really enlightening, challenging and amazing at the same time . . . learning to love like Jesus loved a bit more.'

Team member Adam described a significant moment for his team in a conversation with a friend from their local area who said: '. . . it sounds like you guys are beginning to accept the community, you need to change that around and you need to be accepted by the community.' Adam and his team understood themselves to be the primary actors in their mission, taking the initiative by choosing to move in and accept their neighbours. In telling this story, Adam emphasized its impact: 'That kind of stopped us all in our tracks, you know.' Team members began to realize that they brought features of middle-class culture along with their evangelical spirituality that led to their objectification of those in their communities, described by the anthropologist James Bielo as 'the imagining of a missionalized subject' (2011a, p. 132). But relationships with those experiencing urban deprivation initiated a process of growing self-awareness. In building relationships with the people around them, team members discovered that their new neighbours interpreted reality in profoundly different ways; that they were not simply passive recipients of their activism, but that they too had a voice. Team members began to understand the extent to which community members had been shaped by their urban environments and experiences of deprivation; and, significantly, that they too had been shaped by the stories and places of their own lives. Recognizing her own class background, Sally described the life she and her husband might have lived had they not joined the team:

> . . . I think we probably would have been just living in a little middle-class housing estate somewhere, we wouldn't have known our neighbours, probably would have friends and/or family living miles away, and actually not really have a sense of community. . .

Hannah reflected warmly on the reality of her adopted home:

> . . . people kind of turn their nose up a bit at [this estate] generally who don't live here. [But] people who live here are quite protective over the area, 'cos it's nice actually . . . there is a lot of really good people here . . . initially I thought it was gonna be really difficult, I think because that's what people expect when you move to a more difficult area and I thought we were going to have people vandalizing things, noise and lots of threats . . . and while some of that has happened . . . it has been more positive for me than I thought it would be . . .

Team members have had to re-evaluate their previously held assumptions and develop a new awareness of class distinction and the patterns of inequality that fuel it. Beginning a journey of recognizing class inequality and its impact on communities is a part of developing an understanding of the value of personhood – the fundamental equality and value of all human beings.

Poverty

Alongside class difference, team members encountered real poverty in their communities. Evangelical Christianity has its own particular theological narratives (which we will discuss further in Chapter 5) that shape its approach to engaging with poverty. Much of evangelical social activism is service-orientated, using professionalized models to provide for people identified as being in need (Smith, 2017, pp. 31–2). We might call this doing things 'for' people. For many Eden team members it was this practical approach to social action, and the theological frameworks that underpin it, that provided their starting point for mission. However, through their encounters with community members and their growing awareness of inequality they have begun to question this approach.

The dominant view of poverty in our Western, developed, twenty-first-century UK society is that poverty is lack (Wells, 2015, p. 38). The assumption is that poverty occurs when, either by fault or misfortune, a person or community does not have the resources they need and so outside expertise and resources are required to provide help. Therefore, the appropriate response to poverty is understood to be charity – that those who 'have' give of their surplus to meet the needs of those who 'have not'. This might be described as a needs-based approach and leads to charitable initiatives that offer services or provision to people identified as experiencing poverty.

The theologian Sam Wells challenges this analysis. Rather than poverty as lack, he defines it in terms of isolation – poverty is the separation of people from one another, and is a consequence of injustice (2015, p. 23). If poverty is isolation rather than lack, this changes the way we view people who are marginalized. Rather than being defined by their lack and inabilities, this view suggests that people experiencing poverty already have gifts, skills and resources that need connecting to the needs of others in society. It also implies that there is enough to go around, and it is just that some people are cut off from the resources available. This aligns with a strengths-based approach to poverty, that of Community Development, which is focused on building relationships, drawing out the gifts and resources of communities, and overcoming isolation to address injustice.

Within Community Development, Christian community development and urban theology traditions, the language of 'to', 'for' or 'with' has often been used to differentiate between models. Doing 'to' or 'for' describes needs-based initiatives that maintain a separation between those who 'provide' and those who are 'in need'. Such projects neglect the personhood, gifts and skills of people struggling against poverty and usually simply create dependency. Doing 'with' is strengths-based and recognizes the gift that every person has to bring to their community, cultivating their personhood and agency. Specifically, strengths-based models include Asset-based Community Development, Co-Production, Broad-based Community Organizing, Local Area Co-ordination, Appreciative Inquiry and Poverty Truth Commissions.[3] By acknowledging that all people have both strengths and needs, these approaches to development seek to mobilize and build on the resources and skills of individuals and communities so that they can address their own needs, including campaigning on issues of injustice, or co-designing local services along with policy makers where necessary.

Wells has developed this idea in his articulation of four possible responses to poverty: working for, being for, working with, and being with. His distinction between 'working' and 'being' is helpful. He argues that while 'working with' is good, the nature of work is that it is problem-focused, still seeing a situation as something to be changed. Wells believes that the response to poverty most faithful to the Christian tradition is 'being with', which is about being alongside people struggling against poverty, building friendship, and enjoying the gift of one another's personhood. This, he argues, directly addresses isolation, becoming an experience of reconciliation between people who have previously been 'other' to one another (2015, pp. 109–17).

The Eden model of relocation and long-term commitment provided team members with experiences of 'being with'. Sally described the journey this has been for her:

> When we first came here I was like 'Why have all these people got all these problems, why don't they just, you know, pick themselves up and get on with it?'
>
> . . . everything God's done with me while I've been here has been about softening the edges really and I think that's definitely helped in that process because you just see some of the situations that people face and it can be just quite over-whelming actually . . . and maybe initially that's even a little bit selfish almost because you want to say 'Well, I can help' and 'Look how great we are' . . . but now actually that's less and less important and more and more it's about, you know, this is my community, these are my neighbours, so I need to be seeking them out and getting alongside them and, you know, just being a good neighbour myself and growing the community.

Through the relationships built in their communities, team members have learnt what it means to be 'with' rather than to seek 'to fix', and this has been a crucial part of the loving acceptance and affirmation of personhood that characterizes missional pastoral care and enables life change.

Christian faith and faith-sharing

Alongside class differences, the framing of activity as Christian mission adds an additional dimension of power to missional pastoral care practice, with intentional faith-sharing playing a role in these parabolic relationships. In Chapter 2, I intro-duced community member Margaret and her story of change; I included her description of the way a team member shared his faith as an alternative and challenging narrative:

I bumped into [team member] and he just said you know 'You shouldn't be just behind closed doors, that's not how God wanted us to live our lives' . . . and I thought well, you know, I think you're right, and I'm passing that down to my children that it's OK to live in a cave and that's not how you live . . .

Such words could be heard as an example of proselytizing while she was in a very vulnerable situation. However, the potential of faith-sharing to be manipulative or oppressive is mitigated in missional pastoral care as it is always part of an ongoing relationship, rather than an isolated activity. As team member Dan, in his twenties and from Manchester, puts it:

. . . I've just got to know 'em, that's it . . . just learnt to be there for 'em and then, if they want to do stuff or speak to you about stuff then you can do. But it's just not about forcing anything down their throats 'cos they'll just vomit it back up in your face . . .

In missional pastoral care, respecting personhood by building mutual relationships is a higher priority than explicit faith-sharing, as another team member commented:

I think if we ever think we're here to be missionaries to them then that's not the right attitude to have, because we want to be a part of the community rather than converting them to be us, and even if they find Jesus, well, they need to be them. (Thompson, 2012, p. 55)

Being self-aware about the power dynamics inherent in mission is vital to ensure that mission activity doesn't become oppressive. Again there is correlation with pastoral care in which recognizing one's own 'pre-understandings', which are shaped by ethnicity, gender, class, position and experience, is essential for the pastoral counsellor (Gerkin, 1984, p. 123; 1997, pp. 13–16). Humility affirms the culture and personhood of community members while remaining open to faith stories becoming a part of hermeneutical play and the reshaping of personal meaning-systems. In missional pastoral care, faith-sharing is nuanced, occurring as part of sharing whole personal life stories as relationships grow.

Revisiting incarnation

It is through encounter with people who are different – in class, in experiences of poverty or in faith commitment – that missional pastoral care has emerged with its particular focus on personhood. This challenges the inequalities that can be inherent within relocating mission models. Incarnation has been the driving theological framework for relocation, both for the Eden Network and other similar models. But given that 'moving into the neighbourhood' highlights inequality – or even risks exacerbating it – revisiting incarnation in the light of these encounters is needed to see whether it is able to resource missional pastoral care as a more mutual and egalitarian form of mission. It isn't possible to survey all that has been written on incarnational mission here (see Further Reading for some

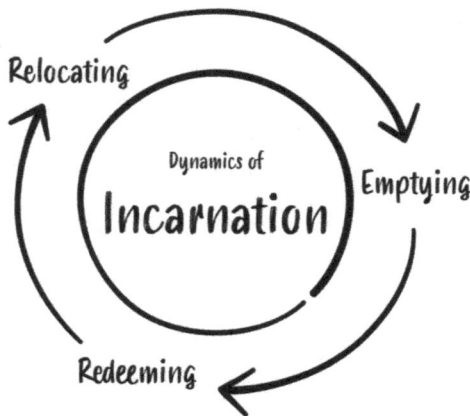

suggestions). However, starting with the experiences of Eden teams and setting them alongside Scripture can help shed some light on the imbalances of power inherent in their activity, and how we might make peace with the awkwardness of difference.

In the early days of the Eden Network, incarnation was understood primarily as relocation. Just as Jesus 'gave up heaven' to become a human in Israel, so volunteers sought to follow him by leaving their (usually) middle-class community and moving house to a 'deprived' estate. Relocation may be a valid facet of incarnation, although it alone does not preclude the kind of pejorative judgements inherent in the language I have used above. In fact, it can be an expression of them – why relocate unless you think a community 'needs you' in some way? But relocation is by no means the end of the story. As team members' awareness of being 'outsiders' – marked by their speech, dress and patterns of living as well as by their Christian identities – grew, so did suspicions about how much of their way of life was rooted more in middle-class culture than Christian faith. This led to some trying to break down these barriers, changing their clothing from jeans to tracksuits, or modifying their speech – a degree of enculturation. While it may be easy to see these attempts as superficial, they demonstrated a growing awareness among Eden teams of the conflicts of identity and a willingness to make sacrifices for their mission. More subtly, many team members questioned how they could be 'themselves' in their mission without alienating those around them, and the Apostle Paul's hymn about the incarnation in Philippians 2 seems to reflect this sense of needing to 'empty' oneself of something in order to become a part of the community:

In your relationships with one another, have the same mindset as Christ Jesus: who, being in very nature God, did not consider equality with God something to be used to his own advantage; rather, he made himself nothing by taking the very nature of a servant, being made in human likeness. And being found in appearance as a man, he humbled himself by becoming obedient to death – even death on a cross!

Therefore God exalted him to the highest place and gave him the name that is above every name, that at the name of Jesus every knee should bow, in heaven and on earth and under the earth, and every tongue acknowledge that Jesus Christ is Lord, to the glory of God the Father. (Phil. 2.5–11, NIV)

Kenosis, or emptying, as a lens through which to understand the incarnation, seems to complement relocation within Eden's ministry. Having moved into the neighbourhood, the effect of difference is to raise team members' awareness of all that they have brought with them, the good and the bad; emptying is a response to this realization. However, this can be misunderstood. What are we emptying ourselves of? And if we see emptying ourselves as the end-point of incarnation, what do we make of Jesus' interventions in the world: his healings, miracles, the resurrection?

For those involved in incarnational mission, emptying can often seem to refer to a need to empty themselves of their personality. But sacrificing our personal identity can actually be destructive. It may sound noble but it can lead to a performance rather than a life; trying to 'fit in' to your community by acting in ways that feel unnatural and inauthentic. Inevitably this is draining rather than life-giving, and ultimately unsustainable over a long period of time. It is important to be clear about what it was that Jesus emptied himself of in his incarnation, so that we can avoid sabotaging our missional efforts with unrealistic and unhelpful self-denial.

In Philippians 2 above, Paul describes Jesus, who is God, not considering 'equality with God something to be used to his own advantage'. In these words we see something about status and something about selfishness. Jesus was 'in very nature God', his status was divine and transcendent. But he did not use that fact to 'lord it over' humanity. He did not behave in a superior fashion – in fact, he added the 'very nature of a servant' to his God-ness. He became human, profoundly the same as others in his community, a son, a brother, a friend. Jesus laid down any sense of exalted status in order to become one with humanity. He also refused to express his God-ness in selfish ways, not 'to his own advantage' but rather to the advantage of others.

Clearly, we are not Jesus. Any correlation we might make between Jesus' incarnation and incarnational mission risks inflating our own importance and missing the mysterious richness of Jesus' life and ministry. But when it comes to the question of how to empty ourselves and become one with our community, Jesus' example shows us that it is more about pride – about status and selfishness – than it is about language, dress codes or personalities. We learn from psychology that it is wholly unhealthy for humans to reject aspects of their characters or identities, as self-acceptance is a part of maintaining the coherent positive life narrative that is so important for us. But it is actually essential for us to empty ourselves of our pride – *our right to be seen as superior to others.*

Any sense of superiority is always fictional; we are one humanity, every person of equal and immeasurable worth, and yet, often fuelled by race, gender and class, those of us born into historically dominant people groups in our societies carry an (often unacknowledged) sense of superiority that oppresses and 'others' people who we perceive as different from – and therefore lesser than – ourselves. For example, this is the way dominant traits such as whiteness become invisible, as the white majority perceive others as black or Asian and themselves as simply 'normal' (Reddie, 2018, p. 6). Because whiteness is perceived to be the norm, it is also familiar – and therefore perceived to be safer, more reliable, more influential and more competent, leading to structural white privilege and structural racism (Eddo-Lodge, 2018, pp. 64–84). Such deeply embedded and usually unconscious biases are profoundly damaging and require an uncomfortable process of critical self-reflection (I might argue hermeneutical play!) in order to bring them to our awareness. Despite discomfort, we need to empty ourselves of this pride in order to rest in our common humanity, respecting one another's personhood with those in our communities – without this, we can never really belong.

The gift of emptying ourselves of our status and selfishness is that we are then free to do the kind of offering of self that we see in Jesus, the third facet of incarnation: redeeming. While Jesus became fully one with humanity, he also offered himself as both fully human and fully God for the good of humanity. The potential for incarnational mission is that we become aware of our sense of superiority and willing to lay it down. We can then freely offer the gifts and talents that God has given us, alongside those of others in our communities, for the good of our common life together. Pears calls this bringing 'one's unique self to the community or situation' and considers the vulnerability of laying down notions of superiority and bringing our real selves as 'a prerequisite for social transformation' (2013, pp. 106–7). Kenosis is not about *not* being yourself, it is about not believing yourself to be better than anyone else. While most of us would say that we don't believe ourselves to be better than others, the unconscious ways that we minimize others betray the truth. Truly redemptive mission is not doing things to or for people such that their agency and potential are minimized and you and your group are confirmed in your superiority. Instead it is coming alongside others as equals, preferring them, bringing what you have and offering it carefully, gently, to add to what they have, enabling a shared redemption for all involved in your community.

By engaging with power in missional practice, and developing an understanding of incarnation as relocating, emptying and redeeming through the lens of valuing personhood, missional pastoral care has led to strengthening of community resilience and, in some cases, community activism. As this team member put it:

> . . . then it's like they join in with you and it's when people join in with you and support the cause that you both believe in and it's like wow this is really collaborative and I never expected it to be like this.

Andrew Grinnell writes compellingly about the potential for relationships such as those formed in missional pastoral care to have a political impact in their neighbourhood and city region

(Grinnell, 2018). Within the stories of the Eden Network there have been examples of shared action leading to changes such as a community playground built on a derelict site and, in one case, an innovative healthcare initiative (Thompson, 2010, pp. 120–4). The logical conclusion of missional pastoral care as a model for mission is solidarity within a community, and just as life change occurs among individuals, there is potential for activism to create change in the neighbourhood as well. In having our awareness raised of the inequalities in communities, there is a challenge not simply to address this in interpersonal relationships but to consider the systemic causes of injustice and seek to bring about change. Missional pastoral care has more to learn.

The combination of difference, locality, availability, practicality, long-term commitment, consistency and love in daily life is shown in the stories of team and community members. This lifestyle creates the kind of relationships in which hermeneutical play can occur, leading to the re-evaluation of existing meaning-systems and experimentation with new ways of seeing the world. However, the questions of power raised by this kind of missional living are not inconsequential; they must be grappled with in theological reflection in the day-to-day living out of faith in communities. Missional pastoral care tells the story of some of that struggle, the desire to find ways of faithful living that enable fullness of life in others, rather than just confirming our status as 'successful helpers'.

Leaning towards mutuality in missional pastoral care raises the question of outcomes – what might happen in people as a result of this kind of mission, and is it what we hoped for? In any pioneering work there is a risk of focusing on the wrong things as 'outcomes' and in doing so failing to notice the richness of what is actually achieved in our mission. If the language of 'transformation' can create unclear or unrealistic expectations for what our missional activity will produce, leading to disappointment, it is important to consider what does happen as a result of missional pastoral care, and ask: What exactly is 'success' in mission?

Notes

1 The Eden Network model of mission is shaped by its Five Cornerstones and Five Distinctives. The Five Cornerstones are:

We are rooted in local church,
We focus on the toughest neighbourhoods,
A large team of people establish their homes in the heart of the community,
Our first priority is reaching youth to see their full potential unlocked,
We belong to a wider relational network.

The Five Distinctives are:
We are incarnational.
We are relational.
We are purposeful.
We are countercultural.
We are holistic. (Wilson, 2012, pp. 212–13)

To read more of the Eden ethos and stories, see Matt Wilson's book *Concrete Faith*, and find other Message Trust publications at www.message.org.uk

2 This is not always easy for Eden teams, however. Particularly in difficult housing markets such as London, team members often struggle to relocate into the hoped-for area and use of accommodation owned by partner churches or hospitality from partner church members or leaders is common.

3 For more information on strengths-based approaches, see the Community Development section of the Further Reading section.

4

If it's Messy, Slow and Complicated, You're Probably Doing Something Right!

As I described in Chapter 1, the desired outcomes for mission are often simply assumed, or articulated in coded language such as 'transformation'. Much evangelical mission is predicated on the hope that people will 'become Christians', understood as a broadly linear journey to a fixed point at which the task of mission is complete. It is usually assumed that this will result in these people joining the church, adding to our numbers at regular services and events. As team member James acknowledged, reflecting on the outcomes of mission:

> . . . You've got the obvious measures, you know, church attendance goes up . . . the main effects are whether or not they become Christians and start living that lifestyle I suppose.

Defining and measuring missional outcomes has been given additional urgency in our current context by the changes in religious practice in British society over the last 100 years or so. Many congregations carry an impression that our once 'Christian' country has now become 'post-Christian'. This might be better articulated as the passing of Christendom – the structural dominance of the Christian Church in UK society – and in lots of ways represents a good thing for the future of Christian faith in our nation as much as for society as a whole. However, it does lead to a sense of fragility, especially within the historic denominations, who are used to being at the centre of British life, not, as they now find themselves, at the margins. For some, particularly white-majority denominations, there is also a very real challenge to survive in the longer term. These factors mean that numerical growth in membership has become a significant priority in evaluating mission initiatives.

Ideas of numerical growth and radical life change shaped the expectations of many of the team members I interviewed. Indeed, this has been the inherited or starting expectation of the majority of people involved in mission with whom I come into contact. A team member I interviewed for an early pilot project described it this way:

> At Soul Survivor when we were sold this big vision of Eden you know 'come in we're going to see loads of young people get saved and everything's gonna change and we're gonna see revival' . . . and then the nitty gritty of Eden, it hasn't been like that. (Thompson, 2012, p. 53)

These words demonstrate a contrast between the language of vision, painted with flair in broad brush strokes, and the language of daily life – the 'nitty gritty' – which suggests a very different picture. The contrast between these two modes of speech is at the heart of this research. Many people engaged in mission begin their work with passion and excitement, inspired and motivated by exactly this kind of vision language. However, the mismatch between this and their missional experiences can lead to some difficult questions, as team member Michael described:

> I came to [this estate] thinking I would see 100 people in our church within about three to five years. We reach towards 70 at the moment 12 years on, we are not there yet . . . some of the more, kind of, holistic side of what God wants to do in people's lives has become more clear to me over the years . . . there's a naivety sometimes, where in our teens and twenties we think that someone making a decision for Christ somehow fixes everything when in fact they may go

back to a messed up home . . . to a drug habit . . . to all sorts
of challenges . . .

Michael rationalizes this tension by framing it as the 'naivety'
of youth; his discovery in mission is that God has a broader
agenda than he first thought, and perhaps that God isn't a
'quick fix' kind of God.

For others it has led to a direct questioning of their effectiveness – remember Sally in Chapter 1, who concluded that 'my
faith is not big enough'. In *Concrete Faith*, his book about the
Eden Network, Matt Wilson includes a number of personal
stories. Among them is that of Ruth Lancey, a former Eden
team leader, who reflects on the results of her time living on
the Valley estate in Swinton. Ruth describes her sense of calling to the Valley estate and God promising that '. . . love will
flow through these streets . . .' She owns the pain of leaving the
Valley in difficult circumstances after eight years, describing
how her 'faith was shaken and questions unanswered'. Ruth
wrestles with her feelings of confusion and failure, but she also
concludes that:

> The Valley may not now be gentrified with middle-class
> Christian clones, but it is full of young men who never did
> end up in prison. And mums who never did commit suicide.
> And teenage girls who never did get addicted to drugs . . .
> and huge families who believe in God, understand why Jesus
> died, and know how much he loves them. (2012, pp. 82–4)

In voicing her disappointment and confusion, Lancey surmises
'. . . maybe the "promise" was not unfulfilled at all, but simply
misunderstood . . .' (2012, p. 83).

This misunderstanding is the gap between the language of
vision and the language of daily life; between coded and ideal-
ized narratives of missional outcomes, and the real journeys of
Christians engaged in mission and those whom they are coming alongside. By celebrating the former and neglecting to pay
attention to the latter, we risk burning out missional workers who are ill-equipped to find God in the realities of their

work. We also risk missing out on the beauty of what God is doing in our world at this time, and the role that we might have to play in it all. In their stories team members were wrestling with these questions and with the emergence of something unknown in their missional practice – something for which they didn't yet have the language, but something that *does* effect change, just not in the way that they had originally anticipated. Missional pastoral care leads to a complex good in the lives of the people involved. While this is different from what Eden teams expected from their mission, I suggest that it is actually amazing, a coming of God's kingdom.

A complex good

A common thread throughout understandings of mission is the hope for positive life change. Whether that is understood to be a change in spiritual beliefs, a reorientation of one's lifestyle towards global justice, or away from drugs – or all of the above – it is none the less life change, intended for the better. Recognizing that change happens through 'hermeneutical play' – the calling into question of personal meaning-systems and experimentation with new ways of understanding the world – highlights that there is both loss and gain in any process of change.

Hermeneutical play is a process that necessarily involves friction; having your perspectives challenged is an uncomfortable experience, even destabilizing. Furthermore, letting go of previously held meanings is itself a loss, even if those meanings were destructive. In life change we take the risk of stepping out of the familiar into the possibility of something better, without really knowing where we will end up and what life will look like in a new landscape. Nevertheless, hermeneutical play is also joyful. Along with the loss of prior meanings is the discovery of new, life-giving ways to see yourself, your relationships and the world around you. There is a playfulness to life change in which moments of 'anything is possible' occur, and the freedom to practise living and thinking differently in daily life leads to new relationships, experiences and personal growth.

The paradox of loss as a necessary part of growth is a central, if often neglected, feature of the Christian tradition; this is epitomized by Jesus' words alluding to his imminent death: 'Jesus replied, "The hour has come for the Son of Man to be glorified. Very truly I tell you, unless a kernel of wheat falls to the ground and dies, it remains only a single seed. But if it dies, it produces many seeds"' (John 12.23–24, NIV).

This positive recognition of paradox is counter to the more prevalent view of loss as negative and gain as success. In this sense we, as the Church, are creatures of our time. Twenty-first-century Western culture is skewed towards quick, clear-cut 'success' and struggles to come to terms with limitation or failure. Wells describes this as a fundamental fear of mortality (2015, p. 36). The technological and medical advances in Western societies since the Enlightenment have, he argues, led to a conviction that whatever the problem – disease, limited resources, death – we can 'fix' it. Wells writes: 'The human project is no longer about coming to terms with limitations and flourishing within them. It is now, almost without question, about overcoming and transcending limitations' (2015, p. 37).

Such a refusal to accept limitation leads, within the context of mission, to only counting the gains as missional outcomes. In addition, we begin to interpret the loss involved in life change more negatively, as something that shouldn't happen, an indication that something has gone wrong. At worst we begin to take it personally, seeing it as our failure because we can't bring ourselves to attribute such negativity to God.

Viewing mission in this way is hugely unhelpful as it paints an unreal picture of life change as an unendingly positive, upward path. This means that we ignore the actual dynamics of change, missing them when they occur because we aren't looking for features such as discomfort, tension and loss. It also leads us to play down the importance of a *process* of change, instead fixating on a positive end-point. In mission this often results in short-term strategies and impact-measurement frameworks that seek only positive end results in a timely manner. Ultimately, our language about mission and outcomes becomes detached from the real experiences of mission practitioners.

For team and urban community members, missional pastoral care has led to a mix of both positive changes in attitude and behaviour *and* loss and ambiguity. Missional pastoral care does lead to personal growth in the lives of both team and community members – it is good, a coming of the kingdom. But inherent to that goodness are threads of loss and limitation – it is complicated! Therefore I describe the outcomes of missional pastoral care as a complex good containing two elements: flourishing and ambiguity. Both are necessary and complementary parts of missional pastoral care and both must be understood as consequences of God's work in the world.

A kind of flourishing

There are five interconnecting effects of missional pastoral care that constitute a kind of flourishing: a stronger love of self, a more positive approach to life choices, an increased ability to act, increasing awareness of a good God, and mutuality. Here is Paul's story:

> I'm not a Christian now but I spend a lot of me time with the Christians . . . I do a lot of voluntary work, yeah, if I'm not in work this is where I am . . . I do get a lot of responsibility off 'em and obviously I appreciate that 'cos it's trust and I am a trustworthy guy . . . it does make you feel good because someone's trusting you with all their property and stuff like that . . .
>
> Say if I carried on on the streets . . . half of us probably be in jail now . . . but knowing these [Eden team members] and starting getting into all more activities and helping out . . . I see my change . . . obviously we still went back to do our own stuff while we was with them but instead of just climb one ladder causing trouble I was climbing two, so I was still messing about causing trouble but also climbing the ladder to gain respect, you know . . . 'cos I was being with them and

then . . . things move on, like, so I was climbing two instead of one, and obviously you only want to climb one ladder and I just jumped back on to the good ladder to go the good way.

God in a way does help you [find] your way through everything if you think about it but I wanna see something before I believe in him . . . God's probably that one rung ahead of me, you know, until actually something happens and I meet up with him, and until that day I'm always going to be one behind him . . .

I could stay away from [the church] for a long time . . . but obviously if I still got to see the people because they're good friends now . . . obviously your friends come and go but these people I've had for eight, nine, ten, some of them . . . 12 years so you build a good friendship with 'em 'cos you know they're always going to be around, so you can trust 'em . . .

Paul illustrates in his own words the complex good in his life resulting from missional pastoral care. Let's take a closer look.

A stronger love of self

First, missional pastoral care leads to a stronger love of self. In case such language makes you cringe or sounds self-indulgent, let me explain. Love of self refers to a sense and acceptance of your own personhood, as I defined it in Chapter 2 – the worth, wonder and reality of your existence; the fact that, whatever else you might be, you are a human being, made in God's image. Far from being selfish, a love of self involves accepting the fact of our worth as a human being, just for existing and, alongside it, the responsibility or significance we carry. As persons we all, for better or worse, make a dent in the world. Therefore our actions have consequences and we are significant. Paul describes 'feeling good' and appreciating the trust he receives from team members as a result of taking responsibility in his volunteer work. This is hermeneutical play in progress; he uses this experience of being trusted to confirm his sense of self as 'a trustworthy guy'. Suzy also described the way that team members trusted her with responsibility at the youth club tuck shop and the effect of this on her self-confidence:

> . . . it boosted my self-confidence quite a lot. Then I started caring about how I was dressed, how my hair was, then people started noticing that *I was a person* (my italics) so I weren't getting bullied as much, and I had friends...

Notice the connections Suzy makes in these few words. She was given responsibility and it raised her self-confidence; as a result of her belief in her own personhood, she began to care for herself in a new way. The response of other people to her changed attitude and behaviour was to recognize that she is in fact 'a person' and to respect her rather than bully her, even to build friendship. By believing in Suzy's significance and giving her space to exercise her personhood, a chain of events was set in motion that resulted in increased self-worth and self-acceptance.

Love of self is therefore the foundation of flourishing. A strong acceptance of one's worth simply as a person leads to making different choices, taking more initiative, daring to believe in a good God, and being able to give and receive in community.

A more positive approach to life choices

Building a stronger love of self contributes to the second component of flourishing: a more positive approach to life choices both large and small. Community member Clare from Greater Manchester articulates this connection:

> I've stopped going out as much, and I mean going out to get drunk and things like that . . . I didn't want to get involved in that because of what I feel . . . not feeling bad but feeling good about yourself.

Clare's words are resonant with Suzy's above; they are about self-care – that is, making life choices that demonstrate respect and compassion towards yourself and that take care of your life, your body and your relationships. Hanley describes the way marginalization leads people to use their choices as a means to assert their autonomy in a social and political situation of helplessness. She writes:

> To feel as though you lack power is to believe that none of your actions has any consequence: which means, perversely, that you give yourself the licence to do what you like on the assumption that it won't matter . . . to let it all go to pieces and not really 'give a shit'. (Hanley, 2017, p. 25)

Making destructive choices is something we all do at times and to varying degrees. It is often assumed that such choices are always made out of a lack of self-control or thoughtlessness. But Hanley's words indicate that what looks like dependence, passivity or an unthinkingly destructive choice is often a response to disempowerment – the sense that we simply don't matter. It is the one option left for us to assert that we have a choice in a context of powerlessness – to reject all of the expectations and requirements of the system that is making us feel helpless. This kind of negative assertion of personhood is the direct opposite of the choices described by Clare and Suzy in response to missional pastoral care relationships.

Missional pastoral care encourages people's belief in their worth as a person and with it their understanding that they are, in fact, significant. This enables people to begin to make choices from the perspective that their actions do matter, that they make a difference in the world, for good or otherwise. Adopting a 'let it all go to pieces' attitude can be self-protective: a form of taking control of a situation in which you feel powerless. But instead, by affirming your inherent significance as a person, another possibility is opened. For Clare and others, it has led to a more hope-filled and engaged way of living. Paul uses the metaphor of climbing ladders to describe this experience for him. He articulates the way in which spending time with team members, 'getting into activities and helping out', provoked him. It enabled him to realize that he was in fact climbing a ladder 'causing trouble', and that there was a different option – a ladder 'to gain respect'. Recognizing that his actions did matter and that he could make a positive contribution to his community through volunteering meant that after a period of climbing two ladders, Paul ultimately chose the 'good ladder'.

An increased ability to act

A further component of flourishing facilitated by missional pastoral care is an increased ability to act, or 'agency'. 'Empowerment' is a term used in many community development contexts to describe attempts to develop greater agency among marginalized people. Equally, the language of 'taking control' is often present in conversations about helping people towards life change. I intentionally avoid both of these terms as for me they present problems in relation to life change. Instead I focus on the language of personhood, significance and agency.

Awareness of one's power, and the exercising of it, is a part of agency, and it can be argued that power-language is especially important among marginalized groups in order to counter the prevailing, unequal distribution of power. However, power can be conceived in unhelpful ways: as individualistic, as power over others, or as invulnerability – the ability to control life's circumstances. If self-worth is built on the basis of our ability to take control of our own circumstances, then it is vulnerable to inevitable and unpredictable *uncontrollable* life events such as illness or bereavement. Ideas of 'power over' circumstances and 'control' are often illusory and therefore misleading. Instead, significance indicates the reality of each person's impact on the world without suggesting control. Significance is about community, not the individual, as we are significant to, and in the context of, the others around us; it is also collaborative and inclusive – my significance does not diminish yours. And significance survives the uncontrollable nature of life; difficult life events may happen, but how we respond and exercise our agency in that situation will make a difference to our experience of it and that of those around us.

In our talk about mission we can ignore the agency of the people we seek to reach out to, focusing almost entirely on *our* actions, *our* capacity to reach, communicate and help *them*. But the natural consequence of a strengthened sense of one's personhood – and therefore one's significance – is not just making more positive choices but making more choices per se. Overcoming passivity and taking initiative, especially in relation to their community, was evident in the majority of community member interviews, often described as a way of 'giving back'.

Community member participants describe new opportunities and expectations for action resulting from missional pastoral care practices. For example, Paul's volunteering called for him to exercise agency while providing the space in which to do so. Equally, Margaret describes a recent conversation in which she took the initiative and offered to help in her community:

> Just the other week I struck up a conversation with [Eden team leader] and I said d'y'know what, I'd love to work on the Eden team at some stage . . . and he said 'Brilliant . . . you'll have to come on board as a volunteer.'

The encouraging response of the team leader to Margaret's offer demonstrates a focus on cultivating agency through practical activity which is effective in enabling positive action.

Community member Helen seemed to lack a sense of her own agency, and in our conversation she often interpreted events as having happened to her, preventing her from moving forward. Despite this, she described her recent thoughts about how she could help others on her estate. Here are her ideas:

> I thought, you know what, I really feel that God's leading me to work with teenage girls and that off the estate, because there's nobody working with the teenage girls; obviously if they leave school they've got hardly no qualifications, some of them drop out of school early, they need to go to

appointments and things like that and just to have somebody who can go to appointments with them and things like that, d'you know what I mean, just coming alongside people.

Helen's story indicates that even in the context of a life in which personhood has not been honoured, it is possible to receive something different. The events of her life seemed to have removed all potential for agency, but through community relationships she is beginning to experiment with a different way of seeing herself and the world.

An increasing awareness of a good God in a person's world

For some of my community member participants, coming to name themselves as a Christian is a part of their life change, but that is not the case for all. As Paul said: ' I don't wanna take that path . . . I don't think it'd suit me that way . . .' To name 'Christian conversion' as a part of flourishing therefore seemed both inaccurate and reductive, as if to say that a faith conviction is somehow compartmentalized in your life. Whether 'becoming a Christian' was part of the story told by my participants or not, they all articulated a raised awareness of God's presence, goodness and involvement in their lives. Paul, despite his determination not to 'take that path', acknowledges with a degree of surprise how significant learning about Christianity and God has been for him. He talked about getting together with a friend and finding God the main topic of conversation:

> . . . it's always the subject we talk about all the time like 'Oh it's mad when this happened' or 'Do you think that's because of that and this is because of this.' It always revolves around, you know, like what God's done or something we've already heard in the Bible or something, and it's like 'It's mad that, you know', and we just spoke about that for an hour . . .

This increased awareness of a good God changes the way that my participants understand the events of their lives, particularly difficult experiences. In this sense it becomes an integral part of hermeneutical play. Community member Kevin described a very difficult time in his life when he found that 'something' had helped him to be prepared to reach out to family who could help him:

> . . . something made me take that number down, it wasn't like you need that number, someone to fall back on, it wasn't like that, it was like you need that number, you've gotta take it with you, so I put this number in my pocket.

Kevin also talked about his interpretation of the story of Lazarus: '. . . it reminds me of, like, when me dad was in hospital, you know, like I was saying . . . he got brought back to life. That's how I relate to it.'

So missional pastoral care involves a broader range of outcomes and a longer-term commitment than might be expected if conversion was the primary goal. As team member Dan puts it:

> This is one of the things that annoys me about the wing of evangelical, Pentecostal stuff which some people can take on is that are you somebody's friend? Are you gonna help them, are you gonna love them just so they make a commitment to God, and if it's not working you're gonna go, or actually even if they don't make a commitment to God are you gonna love them as God loves them, are you gonna just spend time with 'em and just do what God would do for 'em anyway . . .

In missional pastoral care the conventional categories of mission (as reaching out to people before conversion) and discipleship (as supporting new and growing Christians to enter into mission themselves) become blurred. For example, Suzy was 12 when she decided 'I want to know God now' and she had known the team for three years. When I interviewed her she was 19 and the relationships had continued, developing over time. In Suzy's case the relationships that began as mission did not end when Suzy professed Christian faith for herself, indicating a fluidity between mission and discipleship.

Many of the same activities and forms of relationship simply continue to grow, whatever the decision, or lack thereof, concerning a commitment to Christianity. But God is clearly at work. Kevin had begun to include God as a feature of his life, helping him and his family at times of crisis. Paul's curiosity about God was accompanied by a theory that God was 'one rung ahead' of him on the ladder, helping him find his way. While these allegiances may be tentative and uncertain, none the less they represent a form of relationship with a good God who is believed to be present and active, urging them towards a good future.

Mutuality

You will have noticed that the idea of mutuality – a shared participation in community and life change between both team members and community members – has appeared repeatedly in the preceding chapters. Mutuality in missional pastoral care is being part of a community in which everyone is changing. Care is both given and received by team and community members as daily life enables relationships to be formed that go beyond the surface to reveal the challenges and brokenness in the lives of both parties. Team member Sally reflected:

> I'm very bad at establishing new relationships because I do worry about being, you know, too overpowering . . . I think being intentional in trying to establish some relationships has helped me in that as well . . . I would say . . . how accepting people are of you . . . and that they were quite willing to be open and share their lives with you and I thought, well, it's really rubbish if we're expecting that from them, but I'm not going to tell you anything about my circumstances or my situation.

A shared experience of life change consolidates community relationships and brings a sense of creating something new together. Team member Adam recounts the effect of mutuality on him in the context of community activism as he discovered his local residents' association:

> . . . they're one of the best groups of people I've met because they're so desperate to see change . . . it just makes me excited that we're not doing this alone, we're doing this in partnership with people that live in the area already that are already making a change. So I think, you know, when I first started Eden it was like 'We are the people with the answers to the change' but actually people in the community hold the answers . . .

Mutuality is an unanticipated outcome of missional pastoral care. Community members may not have known that they were about to be 'missioned' by Eden teams; but team members certainly did not expect the form or degree of personal change that they would undergo in their mission. Sally went on to describe the way she and her husband have been changed through their experience:

> . . . the sense of community is fantastic . . . we've always had nice neighbours . . . so I think that's probably changed us 'cos I think we would have just come home every night and shut the door and not really thought about anybody else . . . we always kind of reckoned that . . . we would have ended up being just a little cocoon together if we hadn't been involved in these things . . . it sort of forces you to bring people into your home, doesn't it, and to really put yourself in their shoes . . .

This sharing of personal change and community activism was a challenge to many team members' inherited ideas of mission and community. In mission studies, learning from cross-cultural missionaries such as Lesslie Newbigin (1995), Vincent Donovan (2001) and John V. Taylor (1972) has helped to inform recent reflection on mission in a post-Christendom UK. The missiologists Stephen Bevans and Roger Schroeder note the Christendom tendency to see mission as a 'one-way' relationship, with the

Christian bringing a message to the non-Christian. They argue instead for an understanding of mission as 'prophetic dialogue', as 'a style of living in relationship with neighbours' expressed through metaphors such as 'entering into someone else's garden' (2011, pp. 22–33). Recognizing that in mission we are more often 'guest' than 'host' paves the way for hermeneutical play to take place and for all involved to be changed. Combined with ideas of personhood, significance, agency and God's activity in the world, mutuality suggests that the lines between 'recipient' and 'practitioner' of mission are less clearly drawn than we might imagine.[1]

Missional pastoral care as a contribution to well-being

As the previous sections have illustrated, the outcomes of missional pastoral care are too broad to be described simply by 'conversion', which would not be true to the stories of the interviewees anyway. However, as this form of mission is resonant with pastoral care and concerned with positive life change, there are significant connections with theological understandings of human well-being, or flourishing.

The philosopher of religion Grace Jantzen defines flourishing as 'growth and fruition from an inner creative and healthy dynamic' (1998, p. 161); a process of thriving that begins with an affirmation of the world and humanity. Flourishing is incarnational – valuing our physical embodiment as humans and acknowledging our necessary interconnection to other people and to the eco-systems of our planet. In this picture God is immanent rather than distant, the 'divine source and ground' of all creation and incarnate within humanity (Jantzen, 1998, pp. 160–5).

Jantzen's vision of flourishing, with its affirmation of the goodness of the self, confidence in the resources and the agency of the self to grow, and interdependence, is reflected in the effects of missional pastoral care demonstrated above. For me this is evocative of *shalom*, the all-encompassing peace of God, which, as Chapter 5 will show, is an important theological lens to bring to missional pastoral care.

It is with this expansive view that it is worth briefly noting the connections between the flourishing brought about by missional pastoral care and wider non-theological thinking on human well-being. Religion as a social phenomenon is often correlated with well-being in that it is seen to provide practical structures that are of benefit to individuals in times of distress, such as social support, 'a sense of belonging and self-esteem' (Swinton, 2001, pp. 82–3). This may be so, but these factors could equally be true of other social groups and, as the theologian Leslie Francis notes, 'association is not the same as demonstrating causal directionality' (2011, p. 124). Therefore it is important to note both the value of such observations and their limitations.[2] That said, missional pastoral care, with its focus on affirming the self and encouraging agency, is likely to make a significant contribution to a person's well-being.

Public theology seeks to explore the relationship between faith and public life, or society. The public theologian John Atherton draws together the thinking of economists and psychologists to present a list of key contributing factors for well-being: life satisfaction and happiness, spirituality and meaning, positive attitudes and emotions, loving social relationships, engaging activities and work, values and life goals to achieve them, physical and mental health, and material sufficiency to meet our needs (2014, p. 51). The positive self-regard that is at the core of personhood and the ability to act in the world to make changes are pivotal to all of these categories. Whether that be experiencing positive emotions or working to earn the income that we need, human well-being requires a sense of our own personhood and agency. We also need others to acknowledge our personhood so as to join with us in loving relationships and receive our social and political agency in society. The stories of my participants, along with Atherton's criteria, suggest that encouraging respect for personhood, positive life choices and an awareness of a good God through long-term and mutual relationships are supportive of human well-being – flourishing.

Loss and ambiguity

Having explored flourishing as one aspect of the complex good brought about by missional pastoral care, I now turn to its counterpart – loss and ambiguity. Finding a new appreciation of the experiences of loss and struggle in mission is vital to renewing our understanding of God's work in the world. Ambiguity exists alongside flourishing; in fact, they are a part of the same process: hermeneutical play. As Jantzen describes it: death is not to be denied as if it were in opposition to flourishing; it is to be accepted as a natural part of the lifecycle (1998, p. 168). Similarly, Charles Gerkin uses the term 'paradoxical identity' to describe the struggle involved in being human – negotiating the limitations of one's history and present while hoping in the coming kingdom of God (1984, p. 100). Loss and ambiguity are among the effects of missional pastoral care, elements of the complex good and – rather than being wholly negative – they are necessary, enabling the more positive outcomes described above. There are three main sources of loss and ambiguity encountered by both mission practitioners and community members in missional pastoral care: the challenge of living in a marginalized community, the vulnerability of sharing yourself with another person, and the unmaking and remaking of personal meaning-systems in hermeneutical play.

Living in a marginalized urban community

In my earlier discussions of the urban setting, class and poverty, I defined marginality as being left out; this leads to disadvantage – places or people groups who are not given the same consideration, investment and credibility as others. In some urban communities this is expressed in a variety of disabling factors leading to systemic poverty. Under-investment in public transport creates isolation, makes travelling for work difficult or impossible, and undermines social capital as areas become ghettoized from the main thoroughfares of cities and regions. Lack of affordable housing contributes to the fragmentation of communities in which many people are 'priced out' of the places they call home. The rise in low-paid and insecure work (the so-called 'gig economy') means that many need multiple jobs, possibly also combined with benefits, in order to earn enough to live. This paints a picture of people under pressure, often working long hours with additional long commutes to and from work, and still struggling to pay for the basics of daily life.

Understandably, given these circumstances, mental health comes under pressure: stress, depression, anxiety. Poor phys-ical health is often a factor, and over-stretched NHS resources mean that accessing help might be harder than we'd hope. We all have ways to soothe ourselves when we experience times of stress, not all of them healthy. Addictions can creep up slowly, a response to ongoing painful circumstances. Children raised by parents under these kinds of strain are not oblivious; their mental health suffers too. They and their parents are likely to be aware of media representations of 'chavs', 'scallys', 'benefits scroungers'. Such negative stereotypes box you in, leading to a lack of aspiration and struggles in school. Ultimately, your life expectancy is significantly lower if you live in the most deprived communities in the UK than if you live in the least deprived communities (Raleigh, 2019; Office for National Statistics, 2019). Poverty and marginalization are complex, systemic issues, not easily defined or resolved. But they are real, they are usually the result of injustice, and they make life hard.

Often one of the first responses from people hearing about living in a marginalized community is 'How brave'. The stereo-typing of urban communities as dangerous or 'wild' places has been a consistent thread among some media outlets for decades and has had a significant effect on the public psyche (Hanley, 2007, p. 146). This is not to say that crime is not an issue. Wilson describes the early years of the Eden Network in which team members were subject to vandalism, burglar-ies and verbal abuse (2012, pp. 73–4). Team member Michael describes: 'I think that one of the things that is distinctive for me is the actual applying of loving your neighbour even when your neighbour sells drugs or steals from you . . .' While the significance of crime must not be downplayed, Wilson notes that these incidents have become much rarer in recent years (2012, p. 71), and the team members among my participants did not describe any personal trauma resulting from being a victim of crime. Rather, the challenge is relational, seeking to establish connections and authentically living out your faith in situations of distrust or destructive lifestyles. As Michael articulates, crime is a challenge to his understanding of the biblical commitment to love your neighbour.

More likely than being a victim of crime is finding yourself alongside people when tragedy occurs. The statistics relating poverty, health and life expectancy can be difficult to decipher, but experience of living in marginalized communities demonstrates that grief is all too common. Team member Louise referred to the confusion and helplessness she has felt in the face of distressing events in her neighbourhood:

> You have all the experiences that you have to deal with and you think, oh my goodness, what do I even see in this situation, when someone dies or gets beat up by their boyfriend and all sorts of mad stuff, and you don't know what the answers are . . .

Both Michael and Louise connected the challenges of their experiences to their theology, trying to figure out what their response should be. Exposure to the rawness and complexity of life in marginal communities creates tension, ambiguity and loss. Openness to this kind of challenge is necessary if the hermeneutical play of missional pastoral care is to take place, but it is at times a difficult process in which the resultant reshaped meaning-system may be unforeseeable.

Vulnerability of choosing to share yourself with another person

Both team members and community members make themselves vulnerable to one another as they build new relationships and allow one another to see beneath the surface of their lives. As Jan Berry describes: 'the very act of empathy, coming alongside another person and attempting to enter, however temporarily, their worldview and frame of reference, renders someone vulnerable' (2014, p. 209). This adds relational ambiguity to the experience of missional pastoral care.

It would be fair to say that team members were not always aware when they joined an Eden team that vulnerability would be part of their experience. Understandings of mission that focus on doing 'to' or 'for' people often retain emotional distance from those they seek to help. Pity doesn't become compassion for the reason that it lacks empathy – the ability to identify with the state of a suffering person – and so there is no space for mutuality to develop. As we have seen, mutuality is an emerging characteristic of missional pastoral care that is inextricably linked to its understanding of incarnation and personhood. Allowing yourself to be vulnerable with those you are getting to know in your community is a part of building healthy mutual friendships; Sally put it like this:

> allowing yourself to be quite vulnerable with your neighbours . . . actually letting them see that you have got struggles and issues . . . it's important that people see that it's not all rosy just because you declare you're a Christian because stuff happens doesn't it.

As Christians engaging in mission, we can often underestimate, or even remain oblivious to, the vulnerability that we are asking of those we seek to come alongside. If we invite people to share their uncertainties or questions about faith, we are asking something deeply personal and, in responding, people are opening themselves up to our judgement. Clearly respect for the views and experiences of people of all faiths and none must be at the heart of our mission.

The theologian Vanessa Herrick notes that in pastoral care relationships, vulnerability involves choice, the 'voluntary relinquishment of the power to protect oneself from being wounded' (1997, p. 3). While the intentional nature of joining Eden offers team members some control, the vulnerability of community members may be more immediate, rather than a matter of conscious choice. Helen first met a group of Christians when she was struggling with drug addiction. She was very vulnerable in that situation and she describes the time it took for her to begin to trust:

> They used to talk to me and tell me that Jesus loved me and I used to think they were off their heads . . . but then after a while, something inside of me just wanted to know more because they were just always there for me, they showed me love . . . everybody used to say 'Oh, once a druggie always a druggie' and that, and it wasn't the case, you know what I mean, because . . . these people loved me for me . . . and they didn't . . . condemn me or anything for what I'd done, they just loved me and accepted me.

The constancy of these Christians, and their belief in Helen as a person, rather than 'just a druggie', gradually enabled her to build relationships and to see herself differently too. In missional pastoral care the slow development of relationships of trust with team members allows community members to exercise agency and make choices regarding their own openness over time.

This self-exposure is not without risk for both team and community members. Building personal, mutually vulnerable relationships leaves them at risk of harm from one another. This might be in the small-scale insensitivities or disagreements that are a part of most relationships, or in much more serious abuse from people who may have chaotic and unstable lives. As Louise put it:

> I suppose it's trying to get a balance, needing to get wisdom from God because you don't want to be too much on one side but I suppose I was always on the gullible and naïve side and this is a way I have changed really just through working with people. I've just always wanted to see the good and believe the stories and everything and . . . you've just got to

learn the hard way really, which sometimes has been quite hurtful . . .

The Eden Network has robust recruitment processes and safeguarding practices that help to protect team and community members. Developing appropriate safeguarding guidelines is a vital consideration in any community ministry and needs particular attention when the model of mission is informal and relational rather than project-based. Missional pastoral care is ministry that occurs in a community context and that relies upon the support and accountability of a wider local community and Christian community. As it emphasizes the agency and participation of all in mutual relationships, safeguarding becomes a community-wide practice naming the tensions and risks and seeking to share responsibility for ourselves and with our neighbours.

Vulnerability is an uncomfortable experience and we can often be risk-averse, preferring to protect ourselves by 'doing mission to' people we hold at a distance then retreating again to our secure friendships. But the practical theologian John Swinton argues that due to our dependence on others for life itself, vulnerability is the real state of every person (2011, p. 292). He views this positively, concluding that it is at the point of vulnerability that Jesus' incarnation is complete; 'hospitality' – receiving and welcoming vulnerability in mutual relationship – 'is a manifestation of the divine' (2011, p. 293). Vulnerability is unavoidable and is a gift in the sense that, as the sociologist Brené Brown acknowledges, it is the pathway to meaningful relationships, but undoubtedly it requires courage for us to lean in (2013, p. 12).

Vulnerability and support are shared in missional pastoral care, over time, and to differing degrees depending on the life circumstances of participants. The relationships built between team and community members involve both vulnerability and hospitality, and embracing the vulnerability at the core of human experience in this way is courageous. Urban community members and team members risk sharing their lives with people who have very different life experiences from them.

They seek to understand one another and to be understood. While this mutuality goes some way to addressing the risks involved in relationships of care, there is still a need for careful attention to the vulnerability of those involved in mission and those they come alongside (Berry, 2014, p. 211).

Hermeneutical play, the unmaking and remaking of meaning-systems

In Chapter 2, I described hermeneutical play as the core process of life change: re-evaluating and remaking personal meaning-systems in relationships using words and actions. In order for this remaking to take place, previously held meanings must be called into question or even discarded. So, then, loss is at the heart of the very process of change central to missional pastoral care, making the good flourishing we saw earlier a little more complicated. Furthermore, developing a new meaning-system involves taking risks; experiments in new ways of speaking, thinking, behaving and relating need to be tried out, and not all will succeed. Just as learning any new skill involves failing, getting up and trying again, re-evaluating your meaning-system is an ambiguous process, at times involving painful losses, at times great joy, and often uncertainty: feeling out on a limb. It is a slow and incremental lifelong journey, not a quick-fix solution to the challenges we face.

Loss of inherited meaning-systems

Above I quoted team member Louise, who spoke about her confusion in response to difficult events occurring around her in her community. She continued:

> I think my theology has changed quite a bit since coming on Eden. Say it was a nice little pretty box all wrapped up, it's just been opened and has been a bit messy and yeah, you know, not quite as compact and tight . . . it can make you

think 'Oh right, do I believe this just because I have been told it for years and years and I've never had to question it or it's not affected me in a real way?' . . . when it really affects you and someone that you know then . . . it's not quite as black and white.

This is what having your pre-existing meaning-system challenged looks and sounds like. Our meaning-systems are usually neat, designed to make good sense of the world. But they are inevitably limited by the range of experiences we have had personally or been exposed to among the people closest to us. Louise describes the way in which we can easily accept ideas as true if they do not affect us or those we care about. The repetition of ideas in our social worlds over time makes them seem absolute; it becomes impossible to imagine that things might be different. Louise's experience of getting to know and care about different people called into question beliefs that she had previously just accepted. The diverse life experiences of those around her, and the implications of her beliefs for them, caused her to re-evaluate her ideas.

Paloutzian notices that it is when life circumstances are 'inconsistent with deeply held beliefs' that doubt becomes a pressure and motivation to change – when there is a 'discrepancy between the ought and the is of a person's life' (2005, pp. 336–7). This pressure results because of the importance of coherence within our meaning-systems; human flourishing is best served by an ability to connect the disparate threads of our lives, to 'make sense' of them. The difficulty of losing elements of our meaning-system is compensated for by the restoration of coherence once our meanings are reframed to take account of the challenge of experience. Another team member I interviewed put it this way: 'personally I like absolutes, I like things to either be black or white, but I've had to get more comfortable with things being grey areas actually, and even in regard to how people might follow Christianity' (Thompson, 2012, p. 54). Evidently this is a journey and not always an easy path. While this kind of loss might be a disturbing feature of missional pastoral care, and the temptation to protect ourselves may be strong, I believe that God is at work even (and especially) in these destabilizing moments.

The fragility and limits of life change

Following the loss of inherited meaning-systems is the risky task of rebuilding new ways of seeing yourself, others and the world. This rebuilding process is fragile, requiring gentleness and patience – as this observation from team member Adam shows:

> I've seen kids I've worked with going forward for salvation I don't know how many times . . . it just made me think actually is this person saved because they . . . keep respond-ing . . . at first I got a bit annoyed how often kids went forward . . . but actually for them it's them making another stand . . . because it's really difficult for kids in this area to be a Christian . . . coming from an area where your mum and dad kick you out the door at eight o'clock in the morning and don't let you back in until six o'clock in the evening . . . so it is something they need to do again and again if not just to remind themselves what they're committed to . . .

Adam sometimes takes young people to larger Christian events at which they are given the opportunity to go 'forward' in response to a Christian message. His words above hint at an inherent tension in such events. For those hosting the event – the view from the stage – every young person responding is 'getting saved', but for Adam (who lives alongside these young people), what is happening for them is less clear. Adam ration-alizes this ambiguity in terms of 'remind[ing] themselves what they're committed to', which may well be appropriate. There is vulnerability for young people seeking a different identity in their response to Christianity and needing to repeatedly reassert that aspiration. However, Adam's words also highlight his own discomfort with the challenges to his meaning-system concerning what 'becoming a Christian' looks like.

Hermeneutical play opens up possibilities for new self-understanding and new ways of living, but the process of experimenting with amended meaning-systems and integrating new ways of thinking is not easy or fast. Community member Clare's view of her current situation expresses this tension:

I don't think I've completely changed to being a Christian . . . to me you can't just be one day something and one day something else, I mean it might have happened to people, but personally it's not happened to me so I'm going through, like, a bit of a battle so I'm not transformed at the minute . . .

Traumatic life events may play a significant role in inhibiting the adoption of revised meaning-systems. Helen's husband had left her after their conversion to Christianity, and this experience of abandonment cast a shadow over her life narrative – she returned to it several times throughout our interview:

I look back all the time and think to myself . . . when I come out of rehab and the years that were then, we were together and how happy it was . . . until he walked out and left me. It just felt as if . . . everything that God had give us and that we were going through together as a family . . . just felt as if the devil had just took it all away from me in a split second . . .

Helen struggled to find coherence in the events of her life that had been so shaped by the actions of someone else: 'He never ever give me no answers to why he done it'. The impact of events outside of her control led to a continual struggle to find a positive life narrative. Despite this, Helen also acknowledged the role of team members who provided a source of new insight, beginning to call into question the narrative of rejection caused by her marriage breakdown:

I just felt that it was the Lord really just bringing me back, you know, because with Christians and that across my path, and then like since then . . . I've been involved with . . . the guys with the Eden project, doing the kids' club and that with the kids too, . . . being part of the work that they done on the estate where they were cleaning everybody's houses . . . I just feel much stronger and everything now . . . and now I just want to, like, do something now, d'y'know what I mean, and move forward . . .

Ambiguity regarding the lack of, or struggle for, life change is part of the outworking of missional pastoral care. Gerkin addresses this in his work on hermeneutical play as part of a counselling process. He writes that care-seekers often become frustrated as they encounter the limits of their own change, and acknowledges the obstacles presented by traumatic experiences in a person's history (1984, p. 100). For Gerkin, the suffering of the not-yet-fulfilled kingdom of God is a constant feature of human existence, meaning that change will not involve a complete end to suffering. But through the participation of the Spirit, meaning can be reshaped; this allows negative experiences to be re-understood, if not changed and, as a result, a more hopeful way of living can be found (1984, pp. 147–54).

The fragility and limitation of life change is both obvious and unwelcome. It is likely that we can all identify things in our lives and characters that we wish were different. We long for life change and do not receive *all* that we long for. However, in British twenty-first-century culture, never mind Christian cultures, we are not always good at making peace with our limitations. Above I referred to Sam Wells's summary of Western culture as 'orient[ating] people toward solutions, toward answers, toward ways to fix things' (2015, p. 36). In this cultural context, God can become to us the ultimate specialist, able to fix the problems that are beyond the reach of our human abilities thus far. But Wells, and I with him, would argue that problem-solving is not God's primary role in relationship with humanity. In fact God is more concerned with solidarity *with* us than with fixing us (Wells, 2015). By recognizing the fragility of life change as a part of a complex good enabled by missional pastoral care, we open up theological questions about God's character and purpose, as well as cultural questions about the extent to which we have made God in our own, twenty-first-century, Western image.

'Not enough is happening': the slow and incremental nature of life change

In comparison to many forms of mission – and indeed pastoral care – the hermeneutical process of missional pastoral care is more diffuse and may happen over a longer period of time. In addition to being fragile and limited, life change happens slowly, step by step, over time. Arguably, alongside Wells's diagnosis of our culture as solution-focused, we are also often in a hurry; looking for problems to be solved, and fast. Certainly the expectations that many team members held for their ministry included a fairly tight timescale for community transformation. Louise reflected on this as we talked:

> I suppose being here eight and a half years – after two years [wondering] what will it be like when we have been here ten years, there'll be all these amazing stories, which there has been [but] I suppose there are still some you wish you could say 'Oh, there's been this transformation' and there hasn't been and . . . [I] think I am annoyed . . . which has been hard in a way . . . what I can do is pray . . .

The sense that 'not enough' was happening featured in a number of my interviews with team members. It was experienced by them as loss, and was a part of the challenge to their inherited theological narratives, leading to confusion and disappointment. Louise finds it 'annoying', concluding that she can at least respond with prayer; her tone implying a sense of helplessness in effecting the change she wanted to see. Adam related it directly to his reading of the Bible and his own agency: 'We should be doing more stuff out there really, if we got to grips with what the Scriptures tell us then we should be seeing more stuff happen, we should be seeing more transformation.' Using the phrase 'we should' three times in this brief comment indicates the sense of responsibility he feels for what does or does not happen as a result of his ministry.

For team member Michael, who has lived in his community for 12 years, this has tipped over into frustration, although he still frames it positively:

> I would also say on the slightly more negative side is that I simply haven't seen enough of it yet, [I've] got this agitation to see more and a slight frustration with the status quo which I suppose I don't really ever want to lose . . . but I still want to be able to have that joy when it does happen.

These responses can be seen in part as expressions of an understanding of transformation as frequent conversion and quick life change. But they are also a consequence of the long-term and processual nature of missional pastoral care, in which results occur in a non-linear and incremental way.

Missional pastoral care is not a controlled or managed process: the outcome is unpredictable and the path winding. An unintentional process of hermeneutical play enacted in the context of an ongoing relationship may not continue for long enough in order for any remaking of meaning-systems to be established, especially in very transient neighbourhoods. The response of team members to these tensions is the sense of loss described above, coupled with constancy, articulated here by Dan:

> God's out of time, isn't he, so ten years to us is a long time but to God it isn't and the main goal is . . . not an instant thing, it's not an instant commitment, everything's alright; it's working through stuff.

Dan's words are an example of Gerkin's advice to those involved in pastoral care; he suggests that to avoid burnout, care-givers must 'entrust[ing] their identity and the outcomes of [their] efforts to the mysterious working out of the story of God's praxis, God's activity in and through our activity' (1986, p. 71).

Part of the challenge is that we tend to instinctively measure progress in others based on our perceptions of their actions. When we look for signs of change in a person's life we often have a mental checklist that varies depending on our context and the situation. For example, if someone has recently made a profession of faith, we might look for their attendance at church meetings or at a small group as evidence that they are growing in their faith. The difficulty is that our checklists are often subjective and may not be appropriate for the person in front of us; they are also all external – we cannot see what is going on inside a person.

The image of a whale helps me think about life change. A whale travels hundreds of miles under water, but it has to come to the surface to breathe about every 90 minutes. When we see the incredible water-spout as the whale breaks the surface and breathes, we know the whale is there, but the whale has been under the water the whole time. In life change we often focus on and celebrate the water-spout moments but forget that change is happening under the surface, little by little, all the time.

In a results-driven church context the slowness of missional pastoral care can lead to disappointment. When we can see a way forward for someone we care for, we long for them to take that path; but we have to recognize that our view is partial, and respecting personhood means that only that person can begin to enact new insights in their daily life and relationships (Gerkin, 1984, p. 69). If we can understand *why* life change is slow, the process of hermeneutical play, and the significance of constancy, this can help us to manage any frustration and equip ourselves for missional living as a long-term and sustainable embodiment of Christian faith.

Team members express frustration at the slow, fragmentary nature of change in their communities, and community members experience loss and ambiguity as they struggle for life change. But in the face of this, Gerkin concludes that suffering can be understood as meaningful and lived with more positively through grasping our eschatological identity, and that a person's meaning-system 'may be loosened enough to make possible a new horizon of self and world understanding' (1984, p. 154). The loss and ambiguity resulting from missional pastoral care practices are necessary elements of the complex good, as it indicates that meaning-systems are being challenged and subverted, allowing for new understandings of self and others, however partial, to emerge.

Contemporary models of mission frequently fail to take seriously the role of loss and ambiguity in mission practice. The outcomes of mission (where they are actually defined rather than simply assumed) are defined positively – as life change, conversion or societal change, neglecting the loss and difficulty that is inherent within such processes. When loss or pain occurs it is often only recognized in terms of the limitation of life change, and in many instances is interpreted either consciously or unconsciously as failure. This is damaging to both mission practitioners and those they come alongside. It leads to a 'try harder' culture of mission and expectations for outcomes derived more from cultural narratives of exponential success than Christian faith, Scripture, tradition or spirituality.

Missional pastoral care offers a different way to see this; one that can bring insight and hope to all of us who long for life change in ourselves, in others and in our world. It demonstrates that loss or ambiguity in mission is not failure, that sadness or struggle does not mean that mission has necessarily gone wrong. And, perhaps most importantly, that these things are not an indication of God's withdrawal, rejection or disapproval. By recognizing the vital place of loss in the re-evaluating and remaking of meaning-systems that constitutes life change, mission practitioners can hope to persevere through times of grief and struggle in their work, celebrating the processes of deconstruction as well as looking for rebuilding as they and those around them are changed. Those of us who support and enable mission practitioners and communities must also recognize when people need care, and understand that life change can be painful, slow and limited – but that it is nonetheless possible, and God works in the midst of the process to bring about flourishing.

While the headlines of mission rhetoric often offer simplistic or even overly optimistic expectation for outcomes, missional pastoral care demonstrates that when mission doesn't live up to the hype, it is not that something has gone wrong. It is just that people, and mission, are more complicated than our rhetoric suggests. Team members often began their mission with an evangelical expectation of conversion and radical life change – described as 'transformation'. Missional pastoral care has emerged as a different kind of process leading to a different kind of result: flourishing and ambiguity, through mutual hermeneutical play, over time, in the course of daily life. As these expectations for mission are couched in theological terms, inevitably changes in outcomes raise theological questions. Chapter 5 draws out the theological frameworks that informed team members as they began their ministries and the new theological ideas that they have begun to embrace in order to fuel missional pastoral care as an alternative missional lifestyle.

Notes

1 For more on mission in post-Christendom, see the work of Stuart Murray and Paul Cloke and Mike Pears listed in the Mission section of Further Reading.

2 For further work on religion and well-being, including my own previously published chapter on missional pastoral care and well-being, see the Further Reading section.

5

Is Missional Pastoral
Care 'Good News'?

In the previous chapters we have seen the ways in which evangelical Christians seeking to do incarnational urban mission have
moved into a community and found that their hopes for mission
haven't always worked out as they expected. From simply trying
to come alongside others in their communities, a particular way
of life has emerged that I have called missional pastoral care.
And this model of mission has led to some unanticipated outcomes: flourishing across the breadth of a person's life, including their spirituality; loss; and complexity. Eden team members
were seeking to navigate the gap between their expectations for
mission and the reality in which they were living. This gap is not
only apparent in mission practice; it is also often evident in the
theology of mission practitioners and church congregations.

To ask whether missional pastoral care is good news is to
ask: what is the gospel, and where can it be found within missional pastoral care? That these questions are relevant indicates that we have a particular understanding of 'good news'
in mind. If my analysis of missional pastoral care has been generating some questions – or even discomfort – for you, it may
be that it is challenging your inherited theology of mission. In
this chapter I want to explore both inherited evangelical theologies of mission and the theological resources that teams discovered in the course of life and ministry in their communities.
I think that there is a popular 'working theology' of mission
within evangelicalism that is often counterproductive, proving
to be unhelpful in enabling the Christians in this research to
engage fruitfully with their neighbours, friends and commu-

nities. While struggling with this, my participants described the different theological threads that they drew on to resource them in their mission, when their inherited narratives no longer seemed relevant. In these stories we find a richer theology for mission that might in fact be 'good news' in communities.

What they were sent with

> 94% of Evangelicals [surveyed] agree that everyone needs to be born again in order to become a Christian and be saved. 94% agree that people who come to Christ will see their lives transformed. (Evangelical Alliance, 2012, p. 8)

These statistics are the findings of a programme of research into contemporary evangelicalism conducted by the Evangelical Alliance (EA), the leading organization representing evangelicals in the UK. They feature in the report *21st Century Evangelicals: Confidently Sharing the Gospel?*, published in 2012, which presents the views of 1,242 British evangelical Christians taking part in an online survey (EA, 2012, p. 3). Despite the limited size of the group surveyed, the convictions expressed in these statements and the strength of support for them lead to the report concluding that 'It's great to see that the overwhelming majority of us are clear that . . . everyone needs to be born again' (EA, 2012, p. 22). This brief snapshot begins to point towards a widely recognized evangelical missional narrative framing the missional practices of evangelicals.

Evangelical identity has traditionally been defined by its doctrinal commitments. The historian David Bebbington has been an influential voice on the history and identity of evangelicalism. He describes it as a 'quadrilateral' of doctrinal priorities which, he claims, have remained constant throughout its history: 'Conversionism, the belief that lives need to be changed; activism, the expression of the gospel in effort; biblicism, a particular regard for the Bible; and what may be called crucicentrism, a stress on the sacrifice of Christ on the cross' (Bebbington, 1989, pp. 2–3).

This focus on doctrine is one way to understand evangelicalism. But evangelicalism is not simply adherence to a set of doctrinal priorities. It has become a distinct subculture encompassing literature, media, cross-denominational events such as Spring Harvest and New Wine, and public personalities who are aligned not just in doctrine, but in a particular way of being Christian. Organizations and networks such as the EA epitomize and perpetuate this subculture, concerned as they are to define and maintain a distinctively evangelical identity (Guest, 2007, p. 17; Warner, 2007, pp. 31-2). A central function of the evangelical subculture is to shape the story of what it means to be evangelical. We might describe this as an evangelical world view.

Evangelical networks generate narratives, or stories, into which the ordinary evangelical is invited as a way of affirming their religious and cultural identity (Guest, 2007, pp. 197-8; Warner, 2007, pp. 81-5). This is not to say that key leaders or organizations always speak for all evangelicals; many evangelicals frequently engage critically with the views of their leaders (Smith, 2000, p. 7). Nevertheless, identity narratives constitute the backdrop of the faith of 'everyday' evangelicals; they are received as articulating true religious identity and so they must be navigated in relation to the complexity of daily life.

There are also variations and tensions within evangelicalism (Warner, 2007, p. 15). Identity narratives have a different emphasis among conservative and charismatic evangelicals, for example (Guest, 2007, pp. 32-4), and ordinary evangelicals mix elements of the story as they encounter them in different churches or through subcultural events (Smith, 2000, pp. 11-13). The result of this process is what I call a 'working theology', a story about evangelical life and mission that everyday evangelicals accept as authoritative and either try to live into, up to, or struggle with.[1]

Shaping your life as an expression of a particular theological narrative, a story about who God is and how God relates to the world, is inherent to Christianity (and indeed any faith tradition). Being a Christian is to somehow align yourself with your understanding of the Christian worl view. My point here is that there are different versions of the Christian world view, and that aligning oneself with them is often a challenging task. The sociologist of religion Anna Strhan spent time attending a large evangelical church in central London, seeking to understand the evangelical world view. In her research she recognized the tensions church members found between the realities of their daily lives and the story about the Christian life that they were taught in church. She suggests that these Christians found ways to navigate such tensions in a process she describes as 'practising the space between'; strategies included cultivating daily spiritual disciplines, engaging in mutual support with other Christians, and an awareness of a struggle with doubt (2013, p. 237). From an insider perspective we might describe this simply as discipleship: as we grow in faith our attitudes, character and lifestyles become more Christlike. However, it is helpful to take a step back and ask ourselves what we mean by 'Christ-like' and to acknowledge the ways our ideas of the Christian story, and our lives within it, are culturally shaped.

So our 'working theologies' are the everyday assumptions and articulations of Christian faith that ordinary believers like you and me carry around with us. They are a mix of subcultural narratives communicated through sermons, worship songs, reading, Facebook posts, blog articles, podcasts, conference talks and conversations that get collated into a way of seeing the world and God's work within it. These working theologies are often largely assumed, and only articulated in fragments. The result of all of these factors is that they can tend towards being overly simplistic. If we were pressed on a particular aspect of our theology and its implications for our lives, we might admit that things are a bit more complicated than they seem at first; however, these are the theologies that we live with.

Qualitative research, such as that of Anna Strhan and my own in this book, gives us a window into these 'working' theologies. And the account of the world, God and mission described by the team members among my participants was consistent with a broader perspective that felt very familiar, audible and visible through a British evangelical subculture. This coherence, and the way in which my participants described it, led me to begin to call it the 'evangelical missional narrative': the working theology of mainstream evangelicalism that is constructed and maintained by the UK evangelical subculture. This, then, is the theology that the majority of Eden team members carried with them into their urban communities.

The evangelical missional narrative

The lost world

The foundational assumption of evangelical mission and theology is that the world is lost and in need of redemption. Bebbington describes this as the 'three Rs' of nineteenth-century evangelical theology: 'Ruin, Redemption and Regeneration'. Evangelical theology takes fallen humanity as the starting point for a story of salvation from the lost world through the death and resurrection of Jesus Christ (crucicentrism) (2010, pp. 236–7) (1989, pp. 14–16). Within the evangelical world view, Jesus' historic intervention makes conversion available to all, leading to peace with God, a transformed life and a secure eternity (Bosch, 2011, p. 408). The lost world, then, is the setting for the story, creating a clear demarcation between the world and the Church from the start: the lost and the community of faith (Guest, 2007, pp. 2–3).

God and the Church

The central characters in this theological story are God and the Church, who act to intervene in the lost world. God initiates the missional drama by sending Jesus to die on the cross for the sins of the world, and then sends and empowers the Church, effecting salvation for those who respond to the gospel. The Church is the community of converted individuals in a process of ongoing sanctification who are sent by God into the lost world. This sent-ness leads to a Church that is busy, taking an activist approach to mission; Christians and, as a whole, the

Church have a job to do: they work out their salvation in part by sharing the good news of the gospel with lost people in the lost world.

Evangelicals demonstrate a confidence in their own agency, their ability and obligation to impact the world (Bosch, 2011, pp. 10–11). By contrast, in this world view those outside the Church are viewed as passive. Non-Christians are characterized primarily as lost, needing salvation and often moral and social transformation as well (Booth, 1890, pp. 76–7). Their role is to receive and respond to the challenge presented by the witness of the Church. This clearly connects to my earlier discussion of personhood and agency. The belief that the world is lost, and that the Church is the primary agent in bringing the good news of salvation to lost people, leads to mission, including social action, which is 'needs-based' rather than 'strengths-based'. By failing to affirm personhood and cultivate agency, 'needs-based' mission misses a fundamental building block for human flourishing.

A salvation plan

The goal of the evangelical missional narrative is conversion. God sends the Church to witness to God's love for the world and to invite lost people to receive salvation. As Bosch states: 'Salvation does not come but along the route of repentance and personal faith commitment' (2011, p. 410). The activism of Christians in the world both in 'service' and in telling people about Jesus is undertaken to create opportunities for lost people to become Christians. Conversion, or being 'born again', is often understood to occur through 'crisis' or decisive moments. Again, many evangelicals, if asked, may acknowledge that conversion is often a longer process, but the working theology of conversion as a single moment of decision is ever-present as an assumption brought to our mission and discipleship. For example, the EA's report 21st Century Evangelicals contains a section entitled 'Time to decide?', which details the ages at which participants 'made a decision to follow Christ' (EA, 2012, p. 4).

Having received salvation through a conversion experience, within the evangelical missional narrative one becomes a member of the Church and discipleship begins, with the expectation that life change will follow quickly in most cases (Bosch, 2011, p. 343). Commentators on evangelicalism agree that ideas of life change are integral to the evangelical world view (Warner, 2007, p. 18). Arguably, the fact that I have written about 'transformation', motivated by a longing to understand life change in mission, bears this out! Crucially, though, within the evangelical missional narrative, life change is assumed to be linear within the salvation story.

Salvation is understood primarily as being 'saved from' not only one's old life (Coleman, 2000, p. 119; Guest, 2007, p. 3), but also one's old self (Hiebert and Hiebert Meneses, 1995, pp. 373–4; Sremac, 2014, p. 43; Strhan, 2015, p. 68). As a result, it is expected to lead to a dramatic shift in lifestyle and habits as well as attitudes and beliefs. Part of this lifestyle change is enculturation into evangelical subcultural norms such as church attendance, Bible study and prayer both in groups and in a personal devotional time, the 'checklist' I described in Chapter 4. As well as being purely external, such expectations for what it 'looks like' to be a Christian are often the product of an uncritical confusion of cultural values and spiritual values (Bosch, 2011, p. 325). For example, personal Bible reading requires a reasonable level of literacy; attending weekly church or small group meetings requires a lifestyle that is fairly stable and diarized. These factors alone are much more common among middle-class people, and someone with low literacy or who is unused to making appointments may be perceived (and may see themselves) as failing in their Christian commitment as a result of expectations that are more about culture than spirituality.

Evangelical expectation

The final feature of this evangelical world view is a mood of optimism and expectancy (Bebbington, 1989, p. 150; Bosch,

2011, p. 343). There is an expectation that personal transformation and widespread conversion are imminent, sometimes described as a forthcoming 'revival' (Warner, 2007, p. 18). The story progresses with the growth of the Church playing a part in the extension of the kingdom of God, taking another step closer to the fullness of Jesus' reign (Bosch, 2011, p. 430). James Bielo acknowledges different theologies of the kingdom within contemporary evangelicalism derived from various eschatological positions: 'the kingdom is coming', 'the kingdom as now, not yet' and 'the kingdom has come' (2011a, pp. 141–52). These are often mixed and conflated in working theologies. While many evangelicals would describe their understanding of the kingdom as 'now, not yet', the perception of the world as lost and the expectation of imminent transformation in the evangelical missional narrative indicate a working theology that is more akin to Bielo's first category, 'the kingdom is coming', in which the world is considered 'doomed', destined to be replaced by the kingdom of God when Jesus returns (2011a, p. 142).

The evangelical missional narrative is my attempt to characterize the world view that ordinary evangelicals encounter within the evangelical subculture. It can be seen as an example of what the theologian Stephen Crites describes as a 'sacred story', a story through which 'men's (sic) sense of self and world is created' (1971, p. 295). Perceived to be rooted in the authoritative narrative of Scripture, it frames the way evangelicals understand themselves as continuing to participate in the story of God and the world begun in the Bible (Bosch, 2011, p. 532). As congregations and leaders engage with this narrative, it both forms their Christian identity and shapes their missional practice. This working theology illustrates that it is not enough to pay attention to doctrine, as important as that is. Doctrinal commitments become embedded in world views, and combined with social and cultural norms they lead to assumptions, attitudes and actions. In order to understand why we think and act as we do it is necessary to engage with these stories, our personal and corporate theological meaning-systems.

The problem of rejecting context

While this narrative might be widespread, it does seem to be problematic. In a sense, missional pastoral care has arisen because of the mismatch between an evangelical theology of mission and the realities of missional engagement. As with any 'working' or assumed beliefs, articulating them can help us bring them into the light and scrutinize them to make sure that they really are worthy of our commitment. In this case, I think that the difficulties with the evangelical missional narrative stem from a rejection of context.

Context is a much-used word in mission and theology. Context-based leadership training is now widespread, and contextual theology is an umbrella term for a range of liberative theological threads. But a commitment to context can be interpreted in a variety of ways. At its root it simply means the environment or surroundings of a situation. To take into account the context of a comment, action or organization is to appreciate the things that immediately surround it: the times in which it occurs; the habits of speech of those who engage with it; the other actions, words or organizations around and before it. Where differences can creep in is in the nature of the commitment to context; broadly speaking, there are three approaches:

Relevance – Some are attentive to context in order to be relevant. They adopt the language, style or media of their surroundings in order to fit in and communicate well to people in a particular situation. In this relation, the 'context' is passive, and seen as neutral, a tool to be used to reach people.

Opposition – Others are attentive to context in order to oppose it. They focus on its flaws and the damage it is perceived to cause. By opposing this 'dangerous' context, such groups can make clearer their own identity – 'We are *not* them'.

Embrace – others attend to the context in order to embrace it, to learn from it and to acknowledge the ways they are, or might become, a true part of it.

Which of these approaches we take depends on our theology of mission. I think that at the heart of the evangelical missional narrative and its practices is a contested relationship to context, both that of the world (or culture) and the context of the human person (Chaplin, 2015, p. 103; Guest, 2007, p. 3). First, let's consider the world.

In the evangelical missional narrative, lost people are the focus of mission within the context of a lost world. The perception of the world as lost leads to attending to context in order either to be relevant to it, or to better understand its lostness, oppose it, and persuade people that they are in need of salvation. The journey of evangelicalism, as we shall see in the next chapter, has been one of both resistance and accommodation to its surrounding culture, its context. As a 'non-conformist' movement within a wider Christianity, evangelicalism has always been to some extent opposed to the cultural trends around it, adopting what the sociologist of religion Matthew Guest calls a 'paradigm of resistance' (2007, p. 3). The difficulty with such an oppositional relationship with cultural context is that it leads, in practice, to a failure to engage with anyone who is different, and tends towards cultivating 'subcultural isolation' (Warner, 2007, pp. 81–2). Those outside the group are seen simply in terms of their lostness; they are 'othered'. Much of this happens unconsciously, and within evangelical Christianity the non-Christian 'other' is usually viewed with sympathy and warmth, a good-hearted desire for 'them' to become one of 'us'. Over time this perspective naturally creates a subculture expressed in books, podcasts, events and clothing for 'us', not for 'them'.

Every human community, including evangelicalism, is influenced by the cultural trends around it (Bebbington, 1989, p. 271). But its rejection of the context of the world means that it is often not self-aware about the ways it is influenced. This means that it can fail to critique elements of Western culture, such as consumerism or inequality, that might run counter to the gospel. Guest offers this example from his research in a large city-centre-based evangelical church that he calls St Michael's. St Michael's prioritizes conversion and community and capitalizes on the twenty-first-century reinvention of community as networked and trans-local out of a desire to be 'relevant' to its culture. But as more and more aspects of life are co-opted as tools for evangelism, a rich subculture develops that is strongly middle class (2007, pp. 204–5). In his congregational study, Guest concluded that St Michael's 'accommodation to a particular target audience, i.e. mobile, middle-class, evangelicals' is the primary cause of falling numbers and levels of commitment (2007, p. 221). The uncritical adoption of Western middle-class norms led to an insular – and actually reducing – church congregation.

The theological rejection of the context of the world inherent in the evangelical missional narrative can lead to, and perpetuates, a lack of diversity and blindness to the ways we all are creatures of our culture. This leaves us vulnerable to fragmentation between 'us' and 'them' and to unconsciously imbibing elements of our culture in ways that are not life-giving. But there is a second context that is rejected in the evangelical missional narrative: that of the human person, or self.

In Chapter 2, I described the human 'self' as personhood (the value of a human being simply existing) and as subjectivity (our ability to make meaning and a difference in the world through our agency). Identity is the content of what is 'me': the group of values, traits, gifts and skills that I consider to make me, me. A conflicted attitude towards context within evangelicalism equally applies to the context of the person and identity.

The linear salvation plan inherent in the evangelical missional narrative is focused on conversion, involving a rejection of the pre-conversion 'lost' self so that the new 'transformed life' can emerge. Starting from 'lost-ness' is in itself counter to an affirmation of personhood, and Grace Jantzen laments Western Christian theology's focus on sin and salvation rather than the flourishing that she sees as the 'foundation' of Christian faith (1998, p. 157). As the salvation story continues it includes an ongoing suspicion towards the resurgence of that lost self in the journey of discipleship and sanctification. The evangelical theologian Simeon Zahl suggests that converts experience 'private frustrations' at their inability to change. He sees the work of the Holy Spirit in exposing this sin and limitation: 'we die to ourselves again and again, in such a way as to pave the way for transformation and new life' (2010, pp. 88–9).

Evangelical conversion therefore involves recognizing one's lost-ness, cutting off from the old and constructing a new identity. One feature of evangelical popular culture that epitomizes this rejection of self is the telling of testimonies. Most testimonies broadly follow a three-stage, linear process: from life before conversion, through a conversion experience, to life as a Christian. Life before conversion is generally described in negative terms, whether that be dramatic stories of crime or abuse or simply a discovery of emptiness. Conversion is the pivotal point in the story, on which the narrative hinges. After conversion the story emphasizes the positive outcomes of becoming a Christian, the life changes that have resulted. Guest noted this in the culture at St Michael's. He described the oppositional nature of testimony, that conversion is articulated as 'freedom from', and therefore functions to emphasize the badness of the world and the pre-conversion self (2007, pp. 115–17).

Despite the emphasis on this kind of testimony in evangelical circles, for many people conversion is just not as simple as the story we are taught to tell about it would have us believe. We were not 'all bad' before coming to faith and we are certainly not 'all good' afterwards. Furthermore, if we take seriously the nature of life change as a change in meaning-system, then conversion will take time. Remember the analogy of the whale: a whale swims underwater unseen for miles, breaking the surface only occasionally to breathe. Likewise, conversion is a process, punctuated by water-spout decision-making moments, of profoundly changing our meaning-system. So our expectations that linear journeys from bad to good hinge on a dramatic moment of life change fail to do justice to the full experience of conversion.

This is problematic in two ways. First, it is directly opposed to the affirmation of personhood that we have seen is so crucial for human flourishing. If people, prior to making a faith commitment, must be made to understand their inherent badness, then there is less room to affirm them as persons, to love them as they are. Second, it prevents us from maintaining the coherent positive narrative of the self which is so important for human well-being (Gerkin, 1984, p. 69). This doesn't mean ignoring the destructive things we may have done or denying the weaknesses in our character, but it requires that we are able to see these things within a larger story of personal growth.

The evangelical missional narrative when it is preached or discussed in missional contexts – and, often, church contexts – usually begins with a challenge to the self, rather than an affirmation of our personhood before God, and an invitation to see ourselves differently. This leads either to self-protection, rejecting the challenge outright or, and perhaps worse, to self-denial. I don't mean a conscious decision to forgo things like chocolate or caffeine, I mean a (usually unconscious) rejection of our selves. If someone with low self-esteem encounters a stark challenge to their perspective, without an affirmation of their personhood, rather than reject it they may reject themselves instead. This can take the form of 'fitting in', a passive, albeit often enthusiastic, acquiescence to the challenge, which is actually a surrender of personhood. Such a person may seem to adopt faith quickly and dramatically, articulate a complete turnaround in their life and utterly immerse themselves in their new Christian community.

While on the surface this can seem like a good outcome, in the long term such denial of our personhood is destructive and unsustainable; 'fitting in' is faking it. Unless it can gradually mature in time into an authentic acceptance of personhood, 'fitting in' leads to burnt-out and dependent disciples who are not able to sustain their own faith or weather the challenges that life may bring. The theologian Srdjan Sremac describes this as 'false hope' that is linked to a 'fiction' of the self, not the true self. If a convert is unable to integrate past and future selves into a coherent narrative, they may experience 'subjective fragmentation' – distress resulting from the dissonance between the two parts of their life story. They may conclude that their new faith is simply hypocrisy and abandon their Christian commitment – leading to 'de-conversion' (2014, pp. 39–43).[2]

This conflicted relationship to context and to subjectivity is a serious critique of the evangelical missional narrative. But while it has led to Christians engaged in mission experiencing feelings of failure, their mission practice has not been without gift. This theological narrative motivated people to join the Eden Network, which led them into relationship with people they had considered 'lost'. Due, to a large extent, to its commitments to relocation and to marginalized communities, participation in the Eden Network has led team members into a positive encounter with the context of the world and of the self. From their experiences missional pastoral care has emerged and offers a more nuanced model of ministry practice and missional theology; team members and urban community members have begun to develop ways of thinking about God derived from their experiences – and it *is* good news.

What they found there – theological reflection from experiences of urban mission

Deconstruction has not been the only outcome for team members in the challenges of missional practice. In listening to their stories I also heard about the theological surprises that resulted from their experiences. Part of their flourishing has been discovering God at work in ways they hadn't expected. Team members' awareness of a good God active in the world has grown through their involvement in urban communities, and many have leaned into this new revelation. A fundamental change has been from a perception of the world as 'lost' and themselves as bringing God to a place, to a recognition that God is already here at work in people. Building on this conviction, team members and community members demonstrated a developing spirituality that sustains them in their mission, helping them to make sense of their experiences.

This emerging spirituality has four threads: it is defined by the presence and involvement of a good God in the world; it draws on experience as a spiritual resource; it includes reading the Bible for action; and, alongside experience, it is confident that *something* will happen. These theological elements are not in themselves new, but it is helpful to recognize that team members and community members are combining them in a community context to resource a form of missional living and personal life change. Drawing on different theological resources has enabled missional pastoral care to begin to shape an alternative theological story from the evangelical missional narrative outlined above. Where the evangelical missional narrative can be a hindrance to mission, this theology is resourcing it and is enabling the flourishing that comes as a result of missional pastoral care.

God is already here! Missio Dei

Over the last 10 to 15 years it has become increasingly common in mainstream, particularly charismatic, evangelical circles to hear phrases such as 'finding out what God is doing and joining in', or 'participating in the mission of God'. This is the contemporary expression of *missio Dei* theology finding a new place within the lexicon of evangelicalism.

David Bosch traces the history of *missio Dei* as a missiological concept, noting its emergence in the 1930s as Karl Barth and others asserted that mission is first and foremost the activity of God. Bosch summarizes the development of this idea throughout the twentieth century, particularly the clarity it gained as an evolution of the classical doctrine of *missio Dei* in 1952: not only does the Father send the Son and the Father and Son send the Spirit, but the Father, Son and Holy Spirit send the Church into the world. This continued to shape missiological thinking, producing the understanding that 'mission is not primarily an activity of the church, but an attribute of God' (Bosch, 2011, p. 399). The task of the Church was seen as finding ways to participate in the activity of God in mission. Bosch notes that this new thinking was embraced by Christians across the denominations, including many evangelicals (2011, pp. 399–400). He recounts that by the 1970s, *missio Dei* had become a broad and inclusive conception of mission, in which the activity of

God includes 'all people in all aspects of their existence' and is understood to happen through the Spirit at work in human history, not just through the activity of the Church.

This theological thread came to the awareness of the Eden Network primarily through the influence of the missional church movement. For example, the missiologists Michael Frost and Alan Hirsch, in *The Shaping of Things to Come*, first published in 2003, state that they seek to recover the '*missio Dei* – the redemptive mission of God to the whole world through the work of his Messiah' for the contemporary Church (2013, p. 30). They acknowledge that mission is the 'very heartbeat and work of God' (2013, p. 34), and in describing an example of a missional church they write: 'they make the assumption that God is already present and already touching people's lives' (2013, p. 41). The influence of *missio Dei* language on the Eden Network is evident in Wilson's *Concrete Faith*, in which he describes it as: 'the branch of theology that traces the initiative for mission back to the Trinity: God's inner life of love is overflowing toward the world, and he invites us to participate in what he's already doing' (2012, p. 137). He connects this understanding of God's mission with the experiences of Eden team members, writing: 'We invariably find that God has been working by his Spirit preparing the heart of a key local resident long before we ever arrived' (2012, p. 123).

The team members among my participants did not explicitly use the language of *missio Dei*, but their stories included the assumption that God the Holy Spirit is at work in their communities outside of their efforts. Louise referred to a woman from her estate seeking her out to ask about church: 'obviously God was doing something in her, his Spirit was moving in [name] . . .' The adoption of *missio Dei* language by leaders such as Wilson within the Eden Network provided a theological rationale for the urban experience of Eden teams, underpinning their affirmation of the world and the self as sites of God's activity. This has enabled the distinctive character of missional pastoral care to emerge and frames the sense in which it is mission, activity that is understood to enact the mission of God.

A *sustaining spirituality*

With a foundational understanding of God's activity in the world – God's mission – team members, and those of my community member participants who described themselves as Christian, talked about their spiritual lives in ways that were consistent and rich. They shared the everyday spiritual practices and theological convictions that have been significant for them and that together become a spirituality that frames the experience of missional pastoral care and facilitates its meaning-making processes. Team member Michael explains his spirituality as including both mission and prayerfulness, describing an initiative his team did in their community. He said: 'that came from just a prayerful heart so, you know, [prayer] inspires mission and mission drives us back to prayer and in it we have got to be growing as disciples . . .' Michael's commitment to prayer and his own discipleship is integral to his missional lifestyle. He was typical of the team members I interviewed in finding strength and resource for his urban ministry through spirituality, whereas community members looked to God for strength to move on in their lives despite the personal challenges they faced. Four features of this dynamic way of relating to God provide the spiritual backdrop to missional pastoral care as a way of life: a belief in the presence, goodness and involvement of God in the world; finding that God speaks in and through experience; engagement with the Bible as a meaning-making authority; and an anticipation that 'something' will happen.

Defined by the presence and involvement of a good God

Drawing on their *missio Dei* theology, the spirituality of team members is defined by the conviction that God is involved in their daily lives and the communities in which they live. Adam articulated it this way:

> There isn't one situation that's going on that God doesn't know about or God can't sort out, and it's just having, you

know, when you're faced with a situation, it's having the faith that God is above it and that God can work us through the situation to see things change.

Adam's belief in the presence and assistance of God enables him to retain hope for change, navigating the vulnerability produced by missional pastoral care. This connection between God's presence and the potential for change is also picked up by Hannah, who said: 'there's no way we would be here if it wasn't for God and there's no way that anybody on the estate would be transformed at all really . . .' Community members, such as Jack, also demonstrated this awareness:

> I think that the way I've learnt about God, he's there and every aspect of your life that changes it's got God somewhere in there, even if it's you learning about God or God changing you, it's got God in there somewhere whether you realize it or not.

To Kevin, God was present as a listener; he described the way his spirituality was developing in prayer:

> You know you can pray to God and God'll take your problems, all day long . . . anytime I've got like, problems or issues I just pray about it and after I prayed about it, you know, it feels like another weight lifted off my shoulders . . .

For community members as well as team members involved in missional pastoral care, God is present and active, impacting everyday life.

The majority of Eden team members are charismatic evangelicals, meaning that a belief in God's active presence and an expectation that they can hear from God through the Holy Spirit are defining features of their spirituality (Cartledge, 2004, p. 180). This conviction opens up the possibility of God making Godself known in unexpected ways and through unexpected people in daily life. It may even be that this charismatic predisposition has made the adoption of *missio Dei* theology, with its inherent affirmation of context, more likely. Charismatic listening to the Holy Spirit in prayer and *missio Dei* theology come together to enable mission, in that *missio Dei* provides a framework for team members to *interpret* their daily relationship with God: perceiving God at work and seeing the values of the kingdom of God expressed in their urban communities.

Experience as a spiritual resource

A sacramental view of experience has emerged in missional pastoral care as a result of the combination of a charismatic expectation of God's involvement and a *missio Dei* conviction that God is at work in the world, asking us to join in God's mission. If God is at work in the world ahead of us, and we can hear God speak in everyday life, then the experiences of our lives become full of potential for hearing from – and receiving from – the Holy Spirit. In fact, the main task of mission becomes discerning God at work in the situations around us. This may seem a natural development, but it pushes at the boundaries of the evangelical missional narrative. Religious or spiritual experience within evangelicalism is generally understood primarily in terms of conversion and subsequent life change (sanctification or discipleship) (Bebbington, 1989, p. 20; Luhrmann, 2004, pp. 519–20). The expectation of tangible and transformative conversion validates experience as a site of God's action; Guest notes that charismatic evangelical spirituality particularly 'celebrates personal experience as a site of spiritual significance' (2007, p. 105). However, this is often combined with ideas of the lost world and lost people, and so it is generally limited to personal devotional practices or to specific signs or words for others, leading to their conversion (Strhan, 2013, pp. 234–5).

The team members and community members I interviewed had, to varying degrees, found God at work in their experiences. Team members in particular described the ways in which God had changed them through their experience of living in an urban community. Sally has been in her community in Greater Manchester for ten years. She said:

> I think I would say that I'm a lot more understanding of the situations that people find themselves in . . . God's just really enabled me to see that there's so many complexities to life that mean that people find themselves in these situations and actually you just need to get alongside them and just understand that and then find a way to help them to help themselves rather than just being impatient . . . So I think God's really softened me around the edges with that.

Both personally and in ministry, team members have allowed their experiences, understood as the activity of God, to generate insight, including theological insight. Hannah describes the evolving nature of her theology:

> I think one key thing that has changed is the way that I think about the gospel actually, it's evolving still . . . there's a traditional church way of preaching the gospel, that you have to acknowledge that you're a sinner and that you repent and that you come to God and you believe and then you're baptized . . . while that's true I think that round here it's very interesting that there's a lot of people who are in certain lifestyle habits . . . I don't say this lightly . . . But not necessarily of their own volition . . . they really don't know anything else or they've not seen anything else modelled, and they've got very low self-esteem some of them, and to come along and say that you're a sinner isn't necessarily the most helpful to them, so instead of really looking at the behaviours and trying to say look, this is how God wants you to behave, I'm slowly thinking about some of the ways other people do it and it's basically showing God's love and his acceptance, and that he is for them first and realizing that Jesus really does love the sinner.

Hannah's story illustrates the way that her experience has led her to rethink her inherited missional narrative. She believes this to be God at work in her, helping her to understand the gospel in a richer way and better communicate it by 'showing God's love and his acceptance and that he is for them first . . .'. Through life experiences God is working to challenge and change the meaning-systems of team and community members in missional pastoral care.

However, there is, as I articulated in Chapter 4, complexity in the spirituality of team members. Michael described a conversation he had with another mission practitioner about the changes they had seen in their theology:

> Of course we grow as Christians and we are challenged by what we experience and what we see and there will be some shifts along the way . . . [but] I think it can send somebody down the road towards . . . some kind of error if we start sort of muddying it by thinking that our own or their experience is somehow that deep that they change everything, they don't, they just don't.

Here Michael demonstrates some of the tension within an evangelical view of experience. He acknowledges a degree of learning from experience while clearly placing limitations on what experience can bring. Team members are on a journey; they inherited the evangelical missional narrative, and for some this still frames their thinking. It is not easy to adapt to the theological surprises of missional pastoral care; it is a process of loss and ambiguity as well as flourishing. Missional pastoral care is tentative, and new theological understandings are still emerging; but despite this it is evident that for the majority of my participants, experience is not only significant as a spiritual resource, but also authoritative, in that it is perceived as encounter with the active presence of God in the world. Experience has become sacramental, a locus of meeting with God.

Through their own spirituality, team members also draw attention to the sacramental quality of experience in their communities, inviting others to recognize God at work. This dynamic resonates with Gerkin's suggestion that pastoral counselling involves both facilitation of the hermeneutical process of evaluating and remaking meaning; and calling attention to the Spirit at work in the process (1984, p. 71). Sharing spiritual insight derived from experience is one way in which the Christian narrative features in the activity of hermeneutical play.

In missional pastoral care, such 'spotting God' in daily life is not solely orientated towards evangelism, and the mutuality of relationships means that team members do not claim expert status. As a team member interviewed in an earlier project put it: 'realizing that actually sometimes you're better than me, and you really get that about God and I never really understood that before' (Thompson, 2012, p. 56). Team members proactively try to 'point out' or 'call attention to' God, who is already at work; the kingdom is already coming in their community and in those around them, and so their task is simply to draw attention to this fact where it is not yet acknowledged.

Reading the Bible for action and alongside experience

The Bible is central to the evangelical missional narrative, and the use of the Bible within the Eden Network indicates a conviction that the story of God's interaction with the world begun in the Bible continues in the lives of contemporary Christians fuelled by the Holy Spirit. Specific Bible passages have been used consistently by the Network throughout its history to describe the vision and mission of Eden teams. Psalm 37.5–6 and Isaiah 43.18–21 were formational in the early years of Eden's ministry; the image of 'streams in the wasteland' was applied to the Church engaged in mission in marginalized communities, demonstrating the influence of the evangelical missional narrative in its expression of the lost world and the agency of the Church.

But during the Network's history, other biblical texts have been added to this 'canon', demonstrating the shifts in thought and practice at the level of corporate discourse. For example, 1 Thessalonians 2.8, 'Because we loved you so much, we were delighted to share with you not only the gospel of God but our lives as well' (NIV), has become a more fitting description for the practice of Eden teams, demonstrating the broadening of their task from conversion to missional pastoral care. Ezekiel 37.1–10 also became a significant text when it was shared by a team member during a worship service at a Network weekend away in 2005. The story of Ezekiel standing among dry bones and asking God 'can these bones live?' reflects the sense of ambiguity and loss experienced by Eden team members in their emerging missional pastoral care ministry. The passage ends with the dry bones coming to life through the combined activity of Ezekiel, who is instructed to speak to the bones, and the Holy Spirit, who instructs Ezekiel and breathes on the bones, bringing them to life. This is a powerful illustration of the relationship teams perceive between God's initiative in the world and their action. God by the Spirit initiates the action in the story, with Ezekiel seeing God's activity and participating as he is instructed. This is resonant of the *missio Dei* theology and the role of experience that characterize the emerging spirituality of missional pastoral care.

From these beginnings, Bible reading in the spirituality of missional pastoral care has continued to be action orientated. It is a source for missional engagement but it is also read alongside experience, expecting God to speak through both. The 'dialogue' between the 'ultimate author and the reader' (Bialecki, 2009, pp. 143–51) is not restricted to a personal 'quiet time' but is a part of the daily life of mission, becoming a less formal and often incremental process along the way. Team member Michael describes the way his missional practice has earthed the Bible in daily life:

> When I used to think about things like love your neighbour, just a simple, you know, the second greatest commandment in the Bible, I always thought of that in abstract terms because I didn't really know the people next door . . . in that sense I was quite a classic middle-class kid and the thing about Eden is that moving into one neighbourhood where people don't have cars and they don't commute to church

and they can't drive round the country to see an extended
network of friends and family easily and they are quite tied
to one geography, one location, it kind of taught me that
loving your neighbour is abstract but it is also literal and it
is probably literal first before it is everything else . . . it is so
obvious [but] when you come from a background like I do
you miss it . . .

Michael realized that the Bible contains insight and instruc-
tion concerning real, current, daily experience; and that his
middle-class background had insulated him from seeing that in
the past. This shows the way in which experience and the Bible
function together as sources for theological reflection: God's
active presence in experience allows for dialogue, in which different readings of the Bible come to the fore.

Given the dissonance between the inherited theology of team
members and their missional practice, it is unsurprising that
they should look for alternative resources in Scripture to help
them understand their experience. Several team members used
the parable of the sower (Mark 4.1–20) as a metaphor for their
mission. In this story, Jesus describes God as a sower and the
gospel as seed that falls on different kinds of ground; Dan told
it this way:

> . . . [in] a lot of Eden projects, people've made commitments
> and then fallen off and come back and stuff like that but . . .
> when people in the long run, they might struggle with stuff
> but they slowly get their head around stuff, you know, and
> they're more likely to carry on with it because they've took
> the time . . . and it's not been a split, an instant decision and
> after ten minutes or so or a few days, weeks or months they
> go back. It's like that parable in the Bible where you sow
> the seeds and that's all about . . . people's reactions to the
> gospel . . . basic reaction that a Christian makes where the
> seed falls and roots grow up and not where they just have
> a quick reaction 'that's amazing' and then go nowhere or
> where they just concentrate on the worries of the world or
> whatever and just get stressed out and just forget about God.

The picture of ministry created in this passage contrasts with the use of 'streams in the wasteland' from Isaiah 43.19 in which God is seen to change a situation quickly and dramatically. Team members have reflected on both experience and Scripture and, as a result, found alternative resources from within the biblical narrative to resource their mission, making the Bible a part of hermeneutical play in missional pastoral care. When passages that were once meaningful for team members become problematic due to their experience, a new way of reading must be found. In addition, the biblical narrative also becomes an aspect of the parabolic encounter with community members, informing missional pastoral care relationships.

The community members I interviewed had all been exposed to the Bible to some degree, even if just to its shaping role in the lives of team members. But they related to it from a very different starting place, especially as they varied in their degree of interest in, or commitment to, Christian faith. Their use of the Bible demonstrates the influence of team members as they also related the Bible to their own life narrative, as David, in his twenties and from Greater Manchester, demonstrates: 'the whole of Psalm 139 for me as well, the fact that it says time and time again God knows you, he knows where you are, and he'll never abandon you . . .' Community members frequently drew on future-orientated Bible passages, which was striking in contrast with the more immediate use of Scripture by team members. Community members Helen and David both referred to Jeremiah 29.11:

> Jeremiah 29 verse 11 it says, 'for I know the plans I have for you says the Lord, plans to prosper you and not to harm you, plans to give you a hope and a future' . . . I used to always cry when I read it because I used to think, you know, that God has got something for me . . . I used to hold on to that verse. (Helen)

By focusing on the future, perhaps community members are showing their confidence in the constancy of God as they have experienced it through the long-term and consistent commitment of team members in missional pastoral care. It may also reflect a greater understanding and acceptance of the complex good that missional pastoral care produces; that change is ambiguous, involving loss. In Helen's description of 'holding on' to verses in Jeremiah as a source of hope, she is holding together both the flourishing and the ongoing ambiguity resulting from missional pastoral care in an understanding of God's incoming kingdom in her life. Team members were more focused on the initiative of God as an explanation for the sense of *not enough* in the complex good of missional pastoral care. This perhaps indicates their struggle with the long-term and ambiguous nature of their ministry, as Dan concluded: 'God wants to show his love and break through into people but it doesn't take ten minutes, it takes a lifetime . . .'

In missional pastoral care team and community members interact with Scripture as a vital part of the ongoing reshaping of their meaning-systems, finding both affirmation and ambiguity in their relationship with the text. Reading or hearing the biblical text is consistently a part of ongoing personal communication with God, the charismatic 'presence' that enables dialogue (Bialecki, 2009, p. 154).

Something will happen

The final element of the spirituality that sustains missional pastoral care is dynamism, the conviction that something will happen. While this sounds similar to the heightened expectations of the evangelical missional narrative, it has a very different character. Rather than the certainty of an ever-increasing, linear process of radical change, this is an open expectation rooted in daily living in the context of the active presence of God.

Hope for change is maintained without necessarily knowing what that change might look like. The complex good of missional pastoral care has been unexpected, leading to a willingness among team members to admit that they do not always know what will happen as a result of their mission. Ministry is full of odd and surprising encounters that make it difficult to predict what might happen next – for example,

Adam described one occasion with a young person from their youth group and his mum, who had been unable to sleep due to a fear that there was a ghost in their house:

> We don't know to this day if there was a ghost but the point is this lady and her son were petrified of being in the house on their own so we just explained a little bit about the gospel and about God and that God's more powerful than ghosts that are freaking you out . . . we prayed and there wasn't any driving out of demons in the name of Jesus, it was just a gentle prayer of: 'God, what isn't of you would you remove from the house and replace it with your peace and your love', and we saw the woman a couple of days later and she had slept every night since and she felt peaceful . . . So again I don't know if there were ghosts but God did something that night because something, the atmosphere, in the house changed.

This is typical of the ambiguous and open-ended relationships of missional pastoral care in which significant instances occur in the context of ongoing relationships without a sense of where they might lead.

Despite the unpredictability of what may happen, as a result of a theology of God's good and active presence in the world and in them, team members are able to demonstrate confident expectation that God will act even when it is not foreseen or understood. Louise articulates another open-ended story that is shaped by her confidence in God:

> . . . like [Mia] who was on heroin, I have talked about God and I've prayed with her and stuff and we have had some experience of God together, but she has never fully, you know, I don't know where she is with God but she has obviously not walked into the fullness of it and we've not seen that transformation in her life but I am sure anything is possible.

Confidence in God's activism leads to team members understanding their practice as participation in God's initiative, and their expectation that something will happen is based on the

prior work of God. Community members also begin to participate in God's mission as they adopt new practices in the light of
their raised awareness of God's presence. Margaret said:

> Every night before I go to sleep I pray now . . . I pray for certain
> very vulnerable people on here [the estate], there's some very
> vulnerable families and little kids on here and it's awful . . . so,
> yes, it's like all of a sudden instead of the focus being on me
> and my children, which is my priority at the end of the day,
> it's widened my horizons to the larger community . . .

While this dynamic spirituality contains a degree of uncertainty, it is characterized by a confidence in God's active presence and is embodied in daily practices that contribute towards
hermeneutical play. Among team members and community
members, with varying degrees of awareness of God, daily
decisions are taken to align themselves with the good – God's
activity – in their lives and in their communities, trusting that
in doing so, something will happen. As team member Sally put
it: 'God is just constantly changing things, isn't he . . . the
journey's constantly changing, I think that's what makes it so
exciting.' As a result of this dynamic spirituality that recognizes God's active presence in daily life as well as in Scripture,
team and community members are open to receiving the gift
of fresh insight, generating new theology and new practice in
urban communities.

Moving towards an alternative missional narrative

The dominant evangelical missional narrative left my participants ill-equipped to see the gifts of their urban mission or
to engage with its challenges. But as they invested time and
remained open to the new in their mission, different ways
of seeing God, God's relation to the world, and our role as
Christians in mission have emerged alongside new ways to
live missionally. Rather than the lost world of the evangelical
missional narrative, missional pastoral care starts with the

conviction that God is at work in the world. The *missio Dei* is at God's initiative, part of God's own character, and therefore does not start with the activity of the Church; God invites the Church to join God in the world by way of a charismatic engagement with the Holy Spirit in daily life. This has specific implications for missional practice seen in missional pastoral care. First, the activism of the Church is relative to the activism of God; mission is not solely dependent on the action of Christians. Second, God is encountered in experiences within the wider community that include people who don't identify themselves as Christian. As a result, 'lost' no longer seems an accurate description; instead, both the world and the non-Christian are affirmed as spheres of the activity of God.

In missional pastoral care the Bible is a founding story in which it is possible to learn the ways that God acts in the world. It is an authoritative source for theological reflection, including the challenge to meaning-systems involved in hermeneutical play, and is read for action and alongside experience. In its stories, especially those about Jesus' life, death and resurrection, the Bible provides a pattern for life in the world that the Church can imitate. As the Church imitates Jesus, it continues to embody the story of God, which is begun in Scripture. Furthermore, God, as the Holy Spirit, is encountered in people's everyday experience. Rather than limiting spiritual experience to a sign of conversion or ecstatic experiences in charismatic worship, ordinary life experience in the world is sacramental, a means by which God speaks and acts. Therefore experience has a role alongside the Bible in theological reflection and as a part of meaning-making in hermeneutical play.

The conversionist salvation plan of traditional evangelicalism is reframed within missional pastoral care as mutual life change through relationship with those we have previously called 'other'. Difference is foundational to the task of meaning-making in missional pastoral care, team and community members have entered into long-term, significant relationships with those they had previously perceived as 'others', expressed in everyday interaction. Both parties are changed in the course of the relationship, creating a kind of flourishing; missional practice is shaped by the acknowledgement of our own need for change alongside the desire for change in others.

These factors themselves begin to shape a different kind of missional story, but this needs some care. Simply articulating a new 'working theology' and offering it to mission practitioners might lead to another ill-fitting set of expectations rather than a life-giving resource for mission. Perhaps what is needed is not so much a watertight theology (if such a thing were possible) but lenses or approaches to help Christians in mission lean in to the delicate, provisional nature of discerning God at work in our communities. The spirituality of missional pastoral care points to the theological resources that have proved to be helpful and nourishing in the lives and ministries of my participants as practitioners in the context of mission in marginalized communities.

While these different theological resources for mission do provide a (sometimes stark) contrast with the evangelical mission narrative, they are not in themselves new. Furthermore, rather than a complete divergence from the evangelical tradition, my participants are innovating within it: drawing on elements of a broader Christian tradition fuelled by their engagement with Scripture and the Holy Spirit in their daily lives. At the heart of this innovation it is possible to identify some fundamental convictions that have wider precedence within the Christian tradition – convictions about the beginning and the end (or goal) of mission that impact everything in the middle: *imago Dei* and *shalom*. These two concepts are found in different forms across the breadth of Christianity, from mysticism to missional or emerging evangelical. While team and community members are reaching for ideas that run counter to the working theology they were sent with, they are finding threads that weave them into a much older fabric.

Imago Dei

Missio Dei paves the way for revising the view of the world presented by the evangelical missional narrative. Rather than being a lost world, full of lost people, it becomes a place in which God is present and active. Broken for sure, but full of signs of God's presence and gift. Underpinning the idea of lostness in the evangelical missional narrative is that of the sinfulness of the world and of non-Christian people. Our salvation stories frequently start with the fall, in part perhaps influenced by Augustine's doctrine of 'original sin'.[3] Although, when pressed, we acknowledge that creation, including humanity, was initially declared good, our working theologies emphasize the fall, putting the need for conversion front and centre.

The experiences of mission practitioners reveal that rather than lost people, communities are full of people who bear God's image and in whom he is at work. They may have complex or chaotic lives but they still have the capacity for goodness and kindness, and they remind us a little of God in the way they parent, befriend or share. This is not to deny or negate sinfulness, the reality that all of us carry brokenness and speak, act and relate in ways that do not reflect God's goodness and love. Perhaps what is needed is a rebalancing. Rather than starting with the fall and lostness, if we begin instead with God's declaration that creation and humanity is 'very good', an awareness of every person as made in the image of God – the *imago Dei* – opens up a different landscape.

John V. Taylor notes that in Jewish thought, *ruach*, or 'spirit', is distinct from *nepesh*, or 'life-force'. When Genesis describes God breathing into humanity in the beginning, that breath does not confer aliveness but rather personhood (Taylor, 1972, p. 7). Personhood is fundamental to our understanding of the image of God in humanity, what Reddie describes as having the qualities of 'self-definition, transcendence, and agency' (2018, p. 8). Therefore, prioritizing this aspect of our theology can enable the affirmation and respect of personhood which, as we have seen, is so crucial for human flourishing. Furthermore, it makes mutuality possible, enabling team members and community members to share both their gifts and their challenges with one another. By recognizing the *imago Dei* in every person, we build a foundation for missional practice that starts with listening and looking out for a revelation of God in those around us. By first seeing others as 'gift', as a revelation of God and not a theological problem, we can allow missional practice to be shaped by our shared participation, contributing to the life and strength of our communities.

Shalom

The starting point of *imago Dei* enables the building of communities of resilience and camaraderie. The anticipated goal or end point in missional pastoral care is described by team member James as the kingdom of God: 'The whole Bible is about transformation isn't it, it's about God calling his people to live differently, it's about God calling his people to put him first . . . building God's kingdom.' Both evident in the present and always to be fulfilled, the kingdom of God refers to the shaping of human life and society in line with the goodness, peace and justice of God. Holding this language of kingdom alongside flourishing and ambiguity as outcomes of missional pastoral care resonates with the theologian Nicholas Wolterstorff's definition of *shalom*: 'the human being dwelling at peace with all his or her relationships: with God, with self, with fellows, with nature' (1983, pp. 69–71).

A positive view of the world as the location of God's incoming *shalom* is another implication of the *missio Dei*. If we acknowledge that God is at work in the world, then when we engage with society beyond our churches we must be prepared to find God everywhere we go. Rather than overwhelming darkness we instead see pockets of *shalom* in every corner of society, and we are enabled to affirm this goodness as a part of God's in-breaking, peaceful kingdom. *Missio Dei*, then, leads to a rediscovery of the image of God in every person and a new ability to discern God at work in daily life by spotting the emergence of *shalom*, the kingdom of God in the world. Missional pastoral care involves a profound affirmation of the contexts of the world and the person, shaped by a theology of living into the reconciliation and peace that God is bringing out of the world.

The theological evolution seen within missional pastoral care is a distinctive mix. It doesn't simply demonstrate a move away from evangelicalism – for example, replicating post-evangelicalism or the liberal theological tradition. There is something character-istically evangelical about missional pastoral care, not least the stated evangelical commitment of many team members, and I believe it to be good news both within and outside the Church. Missional pastoral care is supportive of human flourishing – that of communities and of Christians in mission. Therefore it may be that it can also contribute towards the continued flourishing of the evangelical tradition in contemporary contexts.

Mission is of critical importance for evangelicals; the ways we understand mission become the ways we understand our own journeys with God. So evangelical identity is wrapped up in its theology of mission – the salvation story I have outlined above. Missional pastoral care is derived from the practical experiences of evangelicals engaged in mission and the people they have come alongside. While this lived wis-dom, with its developing theology, may pose a challenge to mainstream evangelicalism, it is the reality of mission and therefore needs to be taken into account by those who plan and create missional frameworks.

In missional pastoral care, the result of evangelical energy for mission and its charismatic spirituality is a new way of seeing God, the world *and* mission. Perhaps, then, missional practice is the vehicle that can help move evangelicalism forward as a tradition. However, to acknowledge this we need to recognize that it is actually a tradition. Understanding our tribe – how it is constructed and how it might need to change – is vital for main-taining good conversation around mission in the Church and in communities. That is the task of the next chapter: to set this research in the broader context of evangelical faith and practice; and to suggest ways evangelicalism might change so as to keep offering its unique gift to the Church and the world.

Notes

1 Some readers might wonder why I am not using the theologian Jeff Astley's conception of 'ordinary theology' as a way to describe

these 'working theologies'. For the most part, my participants do meet Astley's criteria for ordinary theology in that they have had no formal theological training (2002, p. 3), but working theologies are held by church leaders as much as by lay Christians. In addition, in my view Astley's framework is primarily helpful within the world of academic theology, where it enables professional theologians to hear the views of ordinary people on their own terms. Here my concern is not for the academy so much as it is for mission practitioners, and for many of them, 'ordinary theology' is simply theology.

2 'Post-evangelicalism', a term coined by Dave Tomlinson to describe people who have begun their Christian faith as evangelicals but who no longer find evangelicalism a helpful theological tradition, may also be understood in this context as a form of de-conversion resulting from the failure to integrate the self with a received Christian identity (Lynch, 2002, pp. 37–9; Tomlinson, 1995). For many, post-evangelicalism has been freeing in that the concept has offered them a pathway to question elements of their received Christian identity while retaining faith. For these Christians, a chance to start again in reflecting on who God is and how they might live in relationship with God can lead to a more authentic and richer expression of Christian commitment.

3 The Church has struggled with this aspect of Augustine's thinking throughout its history, and many theologians now regard it as deeply problematic (Fox, 1983, pp. 48–51). However, its impact on our theological thinking is profound, including in ideas of the lost world in evangelicalism.

6

Our Theological Season

Raising the wider questions

So far we have entered into the world of urban mission practitioners and urban community members to see what we might learn from them about God, ourselves and mission. In the previous chapter the flashpoints between urban mission practice and a form of evangelical theology became clear, as I contrasted the evangelical missional narrative inherited by my participants with the threads of *missio Dei*, the image of God in humanity, and *shalom*, which they discovered through their ministries. So then, what do we do with the working theologies of evangelicalism? Are they flexible? Have my participants simply ceased to be evangelical as a result of their experiences in mission? These are vital questions for evangelical Christianity because mission is at the very centre of its identity. Arguably, a focus on God's saving work in Jesus' life, death and resurrection and an invitation to respond to that salvation *is* evangelicalism – its missional narrative is also its identity narrative, its story of itself.

Some might conclude that evangelicalism, along with the evangelical missional narrative, has ceased to be helpful altogether. The label 'evangelical' has often been seen in slightly pejorative terms within wider Christianity and beyond, but in recent years it seems increasingly contentious. In part this is fuelled by the prominence of evangelical leaders in political contexts in the USA. The positioning of evangelicalism in partnership with Donald Trump's presidency has been divisive, with some rejecting evangelicalism on that basis alone and others renewing an evangelical commitment as it coheres with their political allegiances (Davies, 2018). In the UK, ripple effects from the USA have added momentum to existing dynamics within Church and society – the place and role of Christianity in the public sphere, religious diversity, ethical questions of assisted dying and abortion. These, among others, are issues that often highlight the differences between Christian traditions, evangelicalism generally being towards the conservative end of the debate.

The emergent Church and post-evangelical movements clearly articulate the journey of some Christians who, having begun their faith within evangelicalism, now feel unable to continue to identify themselves in that way (Tomlinson, 1995). At its worst, 'evangelical' has been used as a byword for simplistic and dogmatic faith. Some might argue that the tradition is so tainted by this reputation that abandoning the language is the only route forward, but perhaps much of the desire to become 'post' evangelical is the result of the seemingly all-or-nothing ways that evangelical theology and subculture often presents itself: a rhetoric that implies that 'anything other than *our* way to be a Christian is not proper Christianity'.

Of course, evangelicalism is itself extremely broad, with scholars identifying fundamentalist, conservative, charismatic, open, closed, progressive, liberal, missional, emerging and post-evangelical groups (Bielo, 2011a; Bebbington, 1989; Strhan, 2013; Guest, 2007; Warner, 2007). The theologian and sociologist Rob Warner argues that such diversity means that evangelicalism is untenable in the longer term, differences between the various groupings being so great as to be irreconcilable. He suggests that the progressive, open elements will blend into a broader Christianity, no longer calling themselves evangelical; while fundamentalist and conservative elements become increasingly narrow and defensive, losing connection to the wider Church and to society (2007, pp. 230–1). While it is true that this bewildering variety presents a significant challenge to evangelical identity, I wonder, with a little more hope than Warner, whether such complexity might hint at a future for evangelicalism beyond the stereotypes.

Therefore, before we abandon the term 'evangelical' altogether, it might be helpful to take a step back and see evangelicalism in broader perspective, as part of a bigger picture. This in itself is a challenge to the oversimplified 'one way to be a Christian' narrative. But it is vital to set evangelicalism within a wider (and longer) historical, social and theological context in order to understand the contribution it can make to Christian presence in the world. A part of this task is, in my view, to rediscover flexibility and responsiveness within evangelicalism, such that it can continue to adapt and make its distinctive contribution into the future.

This chapter begins with a brief analysis of the complexity of evangelicalism(s), first drawing on the definitions provided by theologians and sociologists of religion and owned by evangelicals themselves, and second, rooting this in an acknowledgement that evangelicalism is a product of its time, both resisting and accommodating elements of modernity and now late or post-modernity. Against this backdrop I offer four features of an evolving evangelical identity: reviewing our understanding of knowledge in the light of our cultural context; moving from a focus on protecting 'right doctrine' to aligning with the incoming kingdom of God; an energetic 'good news-ness' that reimagines missional activism; and a bigger theological story that reshapes and extends the doctrinal priorities of evangelicalism.

The reframing of evangelical identity in missional pastoral care arises from the experiences of mission practitioners who, for the most part, still felt themselves to be evangelical. Their perspectives are supported by others writing about evangelical identity and theology, and deserve consideration from the organizations and churches that make up the evangelical subculture and perpetuate the working theologies that have not proved robust enough to support the mission activity they consider to be a vital part of Christian discipleship. However, we begin with getting to grips with what we mean by evangelicalism.

Evangelicalism as a 'tribe'

Evangelicalism is a tribe. This may sound obvious but it is worth restating. By 'tribe' I mean that evangelicalism is a distinct social and theological grouping within Christianity. What is more, currently evangelicalism is a hugely influential tribe in world Christianity; for example, Justin Welby, the Archbishop of Canterbury – head of the worldwide Anglican Communion – describes himself as evangelical. Despite this influence, it is interesting that ordinary evangelicals are not always aware of evangelicalism's history and development as a tradition. As a lay member of an evangelical church it is possible to have only a passing familiarity with the term 'evangelical', seeing yourself simply as a Christian; or perhaps a 'Bible-believing Christian', committed to New Testament Christianity. This can lead to a forgetfulness of the relationship between evangelical theology and practice and its social and cultural context, in turn resulting in the kinds of theology outlined in the previous chapter. So what does it mean to be evangelical?

What is evangelicalism?

Scholars differ slightly in their telling of the founding story of evangelicalism, with two alternative approaches. The historian David Bebbington presents the dominant view: that evangelicalism is a distinct grouping within Protestant Christianity that emerged out of the revival movements led by Jonathan Edwards in America and George Whitefield and John Wesley in Britain in the 1730s (1989, pp. 1–5). The second founding story is told by evangelical theologians such as J. I. Packer and John Stott, who wrote in the mid-twentieth century emphasizing 'gospel successionism', tracing the roots of the movement back to the New Testament, and arguing that, as the evangelical theologian Brian Harris puts it: 'evangelicalism is essentially New Testament Christianity, as recovered by the Reformation, reinforced by the Puritans and popularized by the awakenings from the 1730s onwards' (2008, p. 202). This emphasis on the long history of evangelical commitments was motivated, at least in part, by a desire to refute accusations that it presented a new or deviant form of Christianity.

The Evangelical Alliance connects both threads in its own definition, written by the theologian David Hilborn. Hilborn describes evangelicals as 'gospel people, committed to simple New Testament Christianity and the central tenets of apostolic faith, rather than to later ecclesiastical accretions'. He traces the history from the Reformation which, he claims, defined 'the theological foundations of evangelicalism' and during which the term 'evangelical' was first used of a group within Christianity. However, he goes on to affirm the work of David Bebbington, recognizing that evangelicalism's 'specific social and historical character did not decisively mesh together until the 1730s', picking up the story as told by Bebbington of eighteenth-century revivalism (Hilborn, 2019).

Having briefly explored the origins of evangelicalism, the task of defining it comes to the fore, and again David Bebbington is the pre-eminent voice whose 'quadrilateral of priorities' mentioned in Chapter 5 – conversionism, activism, biblicism and crucicentrism – provide the starting point for most commentators on evangelicalism and so deserve a bit of unpacking here.

Conversionism is central to evangelicalism. Shaped by the Reformation theology of justification by faith alone, conversion is seen as receiving the gift of salvation. In addition, it offers 'assurance of salvation', which in the 1730s was a radical innovation within a Protestantism that believed that you could never quite be sure of your salvation. Some evangelicals expected an immediate, dateable conversion whereas others emphasized a more gradual process. Either way, it was believed that the converted character would, in gratitude, 'work hard, save money and assist his (sic) neighbour' – that is, live a radically transformed lifestyle (1989, pp. 5–9). *Activism* is a further result of conversion, primarily concerned with working for the conversion of others. Prior to the evangelical revivals, Protestant Christianity was generally focused on individual moral conduct, with no impetus for ministers to reach out to others, so the rise of activism (and sheer busy-ness) in evangelical mission was a huge cultural and theological change (Bebbington, 1989, pp. 10–12).

Biblicism in early evangelicalism was focused on reading and communicating the Bible; it wasn't until the nineteenth century that doctrines concerning the inspiration and interpretation of

Scripture developed, such as biblical inerrancy. This divided evangelicals, who still vary in their approach to reading and interpreting the Bible, while all are committed to its centrality for Christian faith. *Crucicentrism* describes an emphasis on a doctrine of the cross, and particularly substitutionary atonement, as central to the salvation story. Again, in recent years this has proved controversial and, arguably, many evangelicals, including my research participants, have rediscovered a theology of incarnation and broader theories of atonement to add nuance to traditional substitutionary models (Bebbington, 1989, pp. 5–16). Despite a degree of fluctuation and nuance, Bebbington asserts that evangelicalism is characterized by the consistent emphasis placed on these four doctrinal commitments throughout its history (1989, pp. 2–3).

Bebbington's work has been broadly accepted as articulating the foundation of evangelical identity, providing a rich starting point that theologians have reworked and amended over time. George Marsden adds an emphasis on a 'spiritually transformed life' (1984, pp. ix–x); Oliver Barclay (1997), Alister McGrath (1995) and Rob Warner (2007) suggest the inclusion of 'Christocentricity': a focus on the person of Jesus Christ. Revivalism is another theme noted by Warner, and John Stackhouse (2002) and Timothy Larsen (2007), among others, draw attention to 'transdenominationalism' – the tendency among evangelicals to prioritize loyalty to the organizations and networks of evangelicalism above any particular denomination. These additions are helpful in naming some important characteristics of evangelicalism, but build on the foundations of Bebbington's work rather than altering his fundamental conclusions.

The Evangelical Alliance itself adopts a combination of Bebbington's and McGrath's positions, and articulates the doctrinal basis of evangelical identity as follows:

Biblicism – Through the Scriptures of the Old and New Testaments, the God who is objectively there has revealed universal and eternal truth to humankind in such a way that all can grasp it.

Christocentrism – God's eternal Word became human in the historical man Jesus of Nazareth, who definitively reveals God to humanity.

Crucicentrism – The good news of God's revelation in Christ is seen supremely in the cross, where atonement was made for people of every race, tribe and tongue.

Conversionism – The truth of the eternal gospel must be appropriated in personal faith, which comes through repentance – that is, a discernible reorientation of the sinner's mind and heart towards God.

Activism – Gospel truth must be demonstrated in evangelism and social service. (Hilborn, 2019)

Alongside the discussion of its defining features, the historian Mark Smith notes that 'doctrinal fence lines', the idea that 'true doctrine can be held and that its holding is not an unimportant matter', are central to evangelicalism as a movement (2008, p. 1). The importance of right doctrine to evangelicals is evident in the creation of various sub-groupings within evangelicalism, distinguishable along lines of doctrinal emphasis, sources of authority and engagement with wider culture.

Conservative evangelicals maintain a strict focus on the Bible as their only source of authority and give rigorous attention to the detail of the text, although in some cases employing more literal interpretations. They tend to practise their faith in a rational, cognitive, word-based manner, emphasizing preaching, right belief and modifying oneself to fit the text. They may be suspicious of emotion and experience and expect to find themselves at odds with wider culture, leading to their prominent role in many ethical debates. Within conservative evangelicalism the Holy Spirit is understood to speak through the Bible, rather than directly to the Christian. This marks a clear distinction from charismatic evangelicals who, as we saw in Chapter 5, believe that the Holy Spirit is a personal guide and conversation partner manifesting in the gifts of the Spirit and a sense of hearing from God within one's personal prayer life, not just through the Bible.

Charismatic evangelicals usually share a conservative evangelical commitment to Scripture, and a conservative stance on ethical issues, but their different relationship to emotion and experience does create different possibilities, as has become evident in the spirituality of missional pastoral care. Open, or progressive evangelicals continue a liberal evangelical tradition in which developments in human knowledge are considered cause to re-evaluate traditional ways of reading the Bible and, if necessary, doctrine. This can be expressed in various ways – such as commitments to environmentalism and social justice, and progressive attitudes towards gender, sexuality or ethical issues such as euthanasia. The central questions that mark out each of these forms of evangelicalism are 'How is the Bible authoritative?' and 'How does faith relate to human experience?'

The importance of systematic schemas of doctrine notwithstanding, evangelicalism also has to be understood, as we have seen it in Chapter 5, as a subculture that creates theological stories of evangelical identity. The theologian Stephen Holmes takes this approach, recognizing that evangelicalism is a popular movement, more practical than doctrinal, and driven forward by 'preachers and hymn writers, not theologians' (2007, pp. 241–2).

Holding the sociological distinctives of evangelicalism, its pan-denominational networks and activities, alongside its doctrinal commitments is vital to fully engage with evangelicalism as a subculture within wider Christianity (Guest, 2007, p. 197; Lynch, 2002, p. 36). As the theologian Roger Olson defines it: 'Evangelicalism is a loose affiliation, coalition, network, mosaic, patchwork, family of most Protestant Christians of many orthodox (Trinitarian) denominations and independent churches and parachurch organizations' (2005, p. 6).

The influence of this evangelical subculture on mission and evangelical identity is evident in the presence of an 'evangelical missional narrative' in the stories of the mission team members I interviewed. This 'working theology' of mission and what it means to be a Christian was derived from the churches, organizations and networks in which team members participated. They mentioned the significance of subcultural networks such as Soul Survivor and Spring Harvest as a part of their theological formation, as well as the vision for mission held by The Message Trust, the pan-denominational umbrella organization of the Eden Network. Doctrinal statements and stories of evangelical identity from within evangelical organizations provide a top-down perspective; the more complex picture is viewed from the ground up, from the practices of ordinary evangelical Christians; and from the reflections of those who don't identify themselves as Christian, who we encounter in our mission.

Starting with the lived experience of ordinary people makes it possible to give attention to the 'messiness' of how people of faith enact their beliefs beyond 'categories of doctrine and spaces of religious institutions' (Strhan, 2013, p. 225). The EA's 21st *Century Evangelicals* research is an attempt to hear something of this local, lived evangelicalism. It reports that there is 'widespread consensus on issues from Jesus to the miraculous gifts of the Spirit to the environment'; that practices common to the majority of evangelicals include reading the Bible, giving money and volunteering; and that 'there are significant differences between Christians who consider themselves to be evangelicals and those who do not.' They suggest that for evangelicals:

> Faith [takes a] more prominent place in life and [is a] key factor in decision making; [the] Bible is seen as authoritative and read often; that evangelicals pray more and believe Jesus is the only way to God, have an emphasis on evangelism and stronger views on right and wrong.

However, they acknowledge that 'the beliefs of evangelicals are not uniform, and uncertainty is common' (Evangelical Alliance, 2011, pp. 4–8).

So in evangelicalism we have a picture of a vibrant, grass-roots movement spinning off in different directions. While Warner thinks that the end is nigh for evangelicalism, Harris argues that its variance and adaptability will mean that it will continue to develop and its influence within wider Christianity will remain strong (2008, p. 212). But as has become clear in the stories of my research participants, there are challenges to evangelical thought and practice which come to light through mission and that need to be addressed if evangelicalism is to thrive into the future.

A lack of self-awareness

These challenges can be boiled down to the confused and conflicted relationship to context, that of the world (or culture),
and that of individualism, which I described in Chapter 5. The
rejection of the world and the non-Christian as 'lost' fails to
take account of the ways evangelicalism is shaped by its cultural context, and our need for a coherent, positive narrative of
our personhood in order to thrive. What makes this especially
problematic is the lack of awareness and reflection on this confusion within the working theologies of ordinary evangelicals,
and the lack of self-awareness in the evangelical missional narrative is reflective of a lack of awareness within evangelicalism
as a whole.

The story of evangelicalism is one of reactivity, beginning
with a response to experiences of God in the eighteenth-century
revivals and to the wider culture of Church and society. As spiritual experience and religious and social contexts have changed
over time, so evangelicalism has developed in response; as
Holmes notes: 'borrowing gratefully sometimes, pausing to
denounce stridently at others' (2007, pp. 225–6). The difficulty
is that it has often failed to admit this adaptive relationship to
culture, certainly at the popular level of evangelical subculture,
and in the working theologies that it offers to ordinary evangelicals (Bebbington, 1989, p. 271).

Blindness to its own cultural construction has been fed in
two ways. First, by a commitment to Scripture alone as a source
of authority, which stands in contrast to the wider Christian
emphasis on tradition as an additional source of revelation. By
cutting ourselves off from tradition we also cut ourselves off from
our own culture and developing history; after all, a tradition is
simply the cumulative perspectives and experiences of people in
the past. Therefore, by rejecting tradition as a source of revelation, evangelicalism makes it difficult to acknowledge its own
cultural, sociological and theological formation in relationship
to the wider Church and world. Second, this has been further
fuelled by the evangelical concern to be seen as 'simply New
Testament Christianity'. Again, this desire to be seen as a valid,

even ideal, form of the Christian tradition has led to a denial of its rootedness in a particular time and place. The importance of experience within evangelicalism has been limited to personal devotional experience and not applied to the wider frame of human thought and practice. So we have an evangelicalism that is fundamentally reactive and often positions itself in opposition to its context, but is reluctant to acknowledge the ways it has been formed by these contexts.

This reticence is clearly not universal and, as befits the sheer breadth of evangelicalism, the evangelical theologian Justin Thacker responds to accusations of a lack of critical thinking within evangelicalism by describing it as a 'straw man' that doesn't reflect the movement as a whole (2010, p. 246). As we have seen, describing evangelicalism as a whole is a difficult task, and so to that extent he is right. However, perhaps his comments reflect his own standpoint as an academic theologian, whereas missional pastoral care highlights the working theologies of ordinary evangelicals. For a movement so defined by its popular expressions and subculture, it is surely essential that the voices of local evangelical Christians, engaged in missional practice, are heard and the twists and turns of their theological journeys understood and appreciated. If evangelicalism is to fulfil its aims in mission, it will require wide engagement, making these stories of primary importance for the future of the Church.

So holding Thacker's critique in mind, but engaging with the reality of evangelical working theologies, how can we understand – and even rebuild – this conflicted relationship to context and develop self-awareness about the ways it forms and changes our theologies? The first question to ask is: 'How is evangelicalism a product of its time?'

Evangelicalism as a product of its time

The picture of evangelicalism's relationship to social context is not a simple pattern of reaction and resistance. Just as our individual meaning-systems are influenced by the cultural contexts of our families, community and wider society, evangelicalism likewise embodies and accommodates the assumptions and world views of its time and place as well as resisting aspects of them (Smith, 2000, pp. 157–9; Strhan, 2015, p. 17; Guest, 2007, pp. 9–16). This accomodation often goes unrecognized, just assumed as being 'the way things are around here'. While we might be able to get some critical distance from it over time, we inevitably bring cultural assumptions to our experiences that are hard to unpick. Within early evangelicalism this accommodation can be summarized in four themes – individualism, a theory of knowledge (epistemology), supernaturalism and pragmatism – that are evident throughout the development of evangelicalism up to the present day.

The history of evangelicalism is also the history of the Enlightenment and of modernity in the West. It is often acknowledged that the Protestant Reformation played a part in creating the conditions for the Enlightenment and the Industrial Revolution, not least in its emphasis on individual piety. This focus on the individual is embedded within evangelical ideas of personal salvation, offering one example of the values it shares with the world view of the Enlightenment (Warner, 2007, p. 13).

Evangelicalism also adopted emerging Enlightenment ideas concerning ways of knowing, or 'epistemology', primarily a commitment to beginning with the evidence of the senses that was becoming central to scientific investigation. Evangelical leaders like John Wesley applied this method of observation and rationality to religious experience and, in time, logic and reason were also applied to the study of the Bible, which was seen to provide the ultimate evidence for theological truths (Bebbington, 1989, pp. 50–4). Evangelicalism came to embody the 'epistemological foundationalism' of modernity – that is, the conviction that 'there must be a common and rational reliable foundation of knowledge which is universally consistent and accessible by rational thought' (Smith, 2012, p. 150). This is often described as 'meta-narrative', and for evangelicals the Bible was seen as the authoritative expression of the meta-narrative of the world, providing a 'universally consistent' and 'rational' body of knowledge. As a result, all critical thinking and reflection was to be subject to the Bible, such that in 1887, Charles Spurgeon was recorded as saying 'there is nothing new in theology except that which is false' (Bebbington, 2010, pp. 144–5). This approach to knowledge (or truth) and to the Bible is a stance based on modernist philosophical ideas that have come under strong critique as we have moved into late and post-modernity.

A challenge to this purely cognitive and word-based form of evangelicalism came as Romanticism began to influence British society in the nineteenth century, bringing a focus on feeling and intuition, nature and history. Within evangelicalism this led to the introduction of supernaturalism in the form of speaking in tongues and 'natural supernaturalism' – discerning the spiritual significance in everyday things (Bebbington, 1989, pp. 78–81). This was an extreme contrast to the Enlightenment rationality that dominated evangelical practice and, as a result, supernaturalism, while influential, had only a limited following.

The fourth feature that profoundly shaped evangelicalism is Bebbington's pragmatism: 'The spirit of the age – flexible, tolerant, utilitarian' (1989, p. 65). This, aligned with evangelical activism, became a willingness to get on with whatever worked in practice within the work of mission, including radical innovations such as lay and female preachers (Bebbington, 1989, p. 66). The cultural threads of individualism, epistemological foundationalism, supernaturalism and pragmatism highlight the push and pull within evangelicalism in embodying and reacting to social and cultural change throughout the period of the Enlightenment and developing modernity. They also offer a backdrop to some of its contemporary ebbs and flows.

Individualism and middle-class consumerism

Individualism has become pivotal to our twenty-first-century Western psyche. We are culturally schooled in perceiving ourselves as autonomous consumer units, curating our lives as we present ourselves to others. This individualism is tied into our economic and class systems. In order to successfully maintain your sense of being autonomous it is necessary to have the financial resources to be independent and to cultivate a lifestyle within which you can host others. Therefore a degree of economic prosperity is needed to fully 'buy in' to individualism, and economic prosperity in Western society involves participating in the market of human resources and consumption – in other words, we offer our human resources for sale on the job market, and with our earnings we consume other goods and services that support and further define our sense of being an autonomous individual.

Guest argues that the development of consumer markets in late modernity 'heightened the prevalence and power of trans-local networks to shape social life and influence social values' (2007, p. 197). He notes the way that religious identity is commodified within the evangelical subculture as networks such as Spring Harvest, Alpha and New Wine have become brands, offering belonging in a similar style to consumer markets. Guest sees this development as critical to the development of evangelicalism in its current form. In his study of St Michael's he describes the way that its subculture 'endorses the social order of the group's membership', being markedly middle class in its affinities and values (2007, pp. 205–6).

This viewpoint has not gone without criticism among evangelicals. More progressive voices such as the theologians John Drane (2000) and Brian McLaren (2007) have acknowledged the unhealthy alliance between evangelical culture and Western consumerism, which leads in some places to large churches in which belonging is reduced to attendance, and community to maintaining an impressive, if exhausting, events programme. James Bielo describes the efforts of emerging or missional evangelicals in the USA to avoid this, reorientating their evangelical faith towards interdependence in communities that are less wedded to middle-class prosperity. Bielo notes that while his participants offer a critique of modernity in this respect they, also embody it in their values and aspirations as middle-class evangelicals, albeit as people committed to trying to live differently (2011a, p. 279).

Epistemological anxiety

As modernity has given way to late or post-modernity, epistemological foundationalism (the belief in a single rational meta-narrative) has also been undermined (Smith, 2012, pp. 150–1). Dave Tomlinson, the author of *The Post-Evangelical*, describes the shift of context in the faith of evangelicals in this way:

> '[D]uring the twentieth century evangelicalism has had to situate itself in the world of modernity . . . Post-evangelicals, on the other hand, are people who relate more naturally to the world of postmodernity, and consequently this is the cultural environment which influences the way they think about and experience faith . . . (1995, pp. 8–9)

This has led to much anxiety among evangelicals about relativism, the loss of truth and the marginalization of religion in public life. Strhan describes the ways that conservative evangelicals engage with the concept of secularism as they perceive it in their city and culture. She observed sermons describing secularism as an atheistic value system that aims to prevent the public communication of Christian faith, leading to the view that secularism is 'hostile to Christians in British political life'. This, Strhan notes, generates a sense of victimhood, anxiety and fear among congregation members, particularly in relation to speaking about faith in public, which sets them uneasily at odds with the Church's injunction that evangelism is an important Christian practice (2012, pp. 208–10).

Embracing other epistemologies (theories of knowledge), questioning the certainty offered by modernist ways of thinking, and reframing a relationship with the Bible have been largely the preserve of open or post-evangelicals, whose faith is sometimes called into question by the more conservative end of the evangelical spectrum. This is a crucial point for missional pastoral care in which experiences of urban community life have come to be accepted as revelatory in conversation with the biblical text. Can mission practitioners embrace different sources of authority, including their own urban experience, and remain evangelical?

Becoming charismatic

The contemporary manifestation of the supernaturalism introduced by the Romantics is the charismatic movement, which began in the 1960s with renewal in the historic denominations and growth of the independent New, House Church and 'Third Wave' movements that followed (Wier, 2013, p. 7). It was characterized by expressive worship, spontaneous prayer, prophecy, and use of other gifts of the Spirit. Rather than purely functional, worship became about personal encounter with God, including healing and, in some cases, deliverance.

Within charismatic services, insight and experience were elevated above rationality and theology, and the emphasis was on a therapeutic gospel of self-expression and inner healing (Bebbington, 1989, pp. 240–4). Again this form of evangelicalism borrowed from, and was an accommodation to, the cultural mood of the time – 1960s Expressionism – with its emphasis on secular psychotherapy, and has continued to provide a Christian point of connection with the expressive threads within Western culture. Arguably, though, the most recent shift towards well-being through mindfulness is better served by the ancient Christian contemplative tradition, and charismatic evangelicalism is having to do some theological work to find its voice in that sphere (Lambert, 2013).

Entrepreneurial flair

The final thread is perhaps the most ubiquitous within contemporary evangelicalism. Activism has continued to define the movement throughout the twentieth century and into the twenty-first, and a particularly pragmatic and opportunistic response to changing culture has led to much innovation, especially in the cause of mission. In the mid-twentieth century the Church Growth movement, initiated by Donald McGavran in his book *The Bridges of God* (1955), brought church planting to the fore and popularized the use of business management techniques in planning and evaluating missional practice (Glasser, 1985, p. 10).

The cultural mood of optimism and exponential growth prevalent in the 1980s and 1990s was also expressed within the evangelicalism of the time, which Warner describes as dominated by a charismatic entrepreneurialism, prioritizing pragmatism over doctrine (2007, p. 237). Entrepreneurial but formulaic approaches to encourage church growth – such as seeker services and church planting – became popular tools in mission circles. Unfortunately, these initiatives rarely had the impact that was anticipated due, Warner argues, to a neglect of context and the resulting loss of connection to the real impulses and concerns of the contemporary people who were the focus of such mission activity (2007, p. 63). Despite more positive models of 'Relational evangelism', such as the Alpha course – which Hunt argues epitomizes 'the church-growth imperative of many charismatic congregations' (2005, p. 77) – Warner concludes that the lack of attention to context meant that expectations of widespread conversion were unrealistic, leading ultimately to disappointment (2007, p. 64); a boom and bust approach to mission comparable to the economic bubble that would burst globally in 2008.

Evangelicalism might be described as 'a complex construct of historical theology, formulated through an often unperceived interaction with its cultural setting, rather than . . . [an] unadulterated, timeless and universally applicable distillation of the gospel of Christ' (Warner, 2007, p. 14). It is a product of both accommodation and resistance to its social and cultural context. Given this, if the working theologies it currently articulates are proving inadequate to the task of mission in contemporary communities, what might be the next step? What does evangelicalism need to retain and what can it afford to lose in order to grow into the future?

Evolving evangelical identity

So far we have seen the way that features of popular evangelical theology – such as the rejection of the context of the 'lost' world, and the linear expectation for salvation from a 'lost' pre-Christian self to a radically reformed Christian self – contribute to the missional narrative that proved so dissonant with experiences of urban mission. But mission practitioners and urban community members have begun to develop innovative theologies in response to their relationships with one another in missional pastoral care. By unpacking questions of evangelical identity above, my hope is that it has become clearer how these theological problems occur, and how the deep roots of theology and culture make it so difficult to change mission practices.[1] For evangelicalism to move forward as a tradition and in its mission, some change is required. The relationships between team and urban community members in missional pastoral care have led to an evolution in their evangelical identity, reconfiguring it in four strands:

- Revising epistemology in response to our time and place.
- Relaxing a concern for protecting evangelical identity, and instead aligning with the incoming kingdom of God in the world.
- Good news-ness: missional impulse and 'passionate piety'.
- A bigger story: reframing the doctrinal priorities of evangelical theology.

Context and epistemology

Despite Thacker's insistence that evangelicalism is well aware of its two-way relationship with modernity (2010, p. 245), it is evident that among some evangelical theologians, churches and networks this is not readily admitted, let alone allowed to inform contemporary evangelical identity (Warner, 2007, pp. 13–14). The problem with this (more or less wilful) blindness is that it prevents evangelicals recognizing that approaches to Scripture are always provisional rather than absolute, and that the development of evangelicalism as a movement is deeply indebted to tradition and culture. In order to move forward, evangelicalism must therefore own its history, understand itself as a product of its time and place and, consequently, begin to reframe its epistemology.

Recognizing the particular way of understanding 'knowledge' that dominated the Enlightenment, and subsequently modernity, can free evangelicalism from its cognitive rigidity and anxiety. It introduces the possibility that the world might be otherwise; that we may not see all there is to see or see it clearly. This is particularly pertinent to how we read the Bible and understand it to be authoritative. Bielo describes evangelical biblicism as the belief that the Bible is 'a collection of texts that tells a cohesive story about the nature and purpose of God, humanity and the unfolding of time'. This story then provides an 'interpretative frame' to bring to any text (2008, p. 10). A modernist conception of truth combined with the scientific method of the Enlightenment has led to a '"common sense" claim that our perceptions can be depended upon as offering direct and reliable knowledge of the world [which] has underpinned evangelical orientations to the Bible as a straightforward and unmediated source of truth' (Guest, 2012, p. 482).

The difficulty in this lies in a lack of awareness of the factors that influence our reading of the Bible. Whether it does point towards an overarching narrative is one question; the other is *which* narrative we find when we read, and how closely it confirms the assumptions of our particular place in society. The question is not whether truth exists, but how able we are to access it. Harris draws on the progressive evangelical theologian Stanley Grenz for an alternative way forward. Grenz emphasizes the 'Spirit illuminated text', by which he means that reading the Bible is a dynamic engagement with the Holy Spirit who brings 'illumination', rather than simply a matter of explaining an objective text, enabling an openness in biblical interpretation (Grenz, 1994).

Reframing evangelical epistemology from a fixed, rigid idea of revealed truth to a fluid, expansive embrace of truth as revealed *and* being revealed allows for greater consistency in more charismatic quarters of evangelicalism where the revelation of spiritual experiences, such as hearing from God and receiving healing, are already considered authoritative to a large extent. The activity of the Holy Spirit in the Christian life means that personal experience, the corporate experiences of the Christian tradition and our cultural context all become potential sites of God's action and voice alongside Scripture. Doing theology, then, is an open and fluid conversation between these different sources of insight, discerning God at work and allowing ourselves to be challenged and changed along the way. The emerging theologies found in missional pastoral care have arisen through just this kind of process as team and community members discovered that God was at work in unexpected ways and through unexpected people.

A shift in epistemology is therefore a natural extension of *missio Dei* theology, as it expands the sense of God at work, by the Holy Spirit, from the personal devotional life of the Christian to mission within the world. John V. Taylor argued that without a *missio Dei* understanding of the work of the Holy Spirit, mission becomes focused only on the agency and obligation of the Christian with an 'it all depends on me' attitude (1972, p. 3). For Taylor, the *missio Dei* happens as the Holy Spirit works in the world to enable transcendent experiences of awareness of an 'other' or of a 'greater whole'; to enable and require people to make personal and responsible choices; and to call out of people 'self-oblation and sacrifice' (1972, p. 39). For evangelicals in mission this opens up the possibility that God can speak and work through people and institutions outside the Church who may claim another faith or no faith at all. It also demonstrates that God's mission is not just from the Christian to the not-yet-Christian; rather, God is working out God's mission in the world in both Christians and those who don't call themselves Christian. We are all the focus of the mission of God to usher in *shalom* in the world.

Letting go – from protecting 'right doctrine' to aligning with the incoming kingdom

We saw earlier in this chapter the importance of defining theological boundaries within evangelicalism. The patterns of resistance *and* accommodation to wider cultures of both Church and world have been of such significance for evangelicalism as a movement that Christian Smith concludes that it is this struggle for self-definition through a 'passionate engagement' with culture that maintains evangelical identity (Smith, 1998, p. 89; Guest, 2007, p. 16).

Resistance and accommodation to cultural context are still evident within missional pastoral care, but they are directed differently. Missional pastoral care involves an embrace of context: that of the world and the individual. This is a form of accommodation in that team members seek out and align themselves with the good – that which reflects the character or activity of God – in a community, person or situation; as team member Adam demonstrates: 'It's not just people moving into the area that wanna change the area, there are people dotted around the streets that have the same heart as us.' This positivity and sense of shared endeavour in community is affirmed by the evangelical theologian Nigel Biggar's distinction between the 'World' as a proper noun, a metaphor indicating a sphere that is hostile to the Church, and the 'actual world', which is not always hostile. He argues that 'as the world is not always the World', it follows that churches are not, and should not, always be separate from it (2011, p. 9). The reflections of my participants resonate with this shift in theology, towards an evangelicalism that recognizes itself as part of, and one with, its community and society.

Resistance to contemporary culture is seen in the explicit rejection of destructive behaviours such as alcohol and drug abuse, violence, and gossip within missional pastoral care. Team member Dan describes this countercultural stance:

> They [the young people he befriended] knew certain morals . . . so they knew . . . you don't believe in stuff like swearing and slagging people off and gossiping about people and all that stuff, but they . . . knew that we accepted and cared about 'em but that we've got different . . . beliefs.

Michael further illustrates the way that teams seek to resist destructive behaviours in his description of a recent conversation with a recovering alcoholic man in his community:

> He said he doesn't think he would have been alive if we hadn't been around when he was at the bottom of his pit of drinking and seemed completely without hope, and he said that what he needed was friends to pick him up, not to treat him like a project, but friends who would pick him up and try and help him to keep going with his life and not to give up, and to work towards quitting drinking . . .

There is also resistance towards excessive consumerism, unfair trading practices, poverty, injustice and environmental crises, both within their own communities and further afield. Team member James describes his involvement in Eden as: 'dedication to a group in society that society's happy to forget about . . .'.

It is a theology of the kingdom – or *shalom* – that provides a different focus for resistance and accommodation in missional pastoral care. Team members try to overcome what is destructive of *shalom* while strengthening the good. This leads to opposition to certain behaviours and aspects of culture, alongside a positive intention to build on (and with) the good in others and in their communities. Attention to the incoming kingdom of God becomes more important than protecting or defining a Christian identity, as team member Hannah describes:

> it's not like an organizational focus . . . the team is made up of a huge mix of people who come from a lot of different backgrounds and it reminds me of being on a mission campus rather than . . . being in a church, so while you've got obstacles to overcome from that situation 'cos you've got a lot of things you think slightly differently about, it's again as a team your focus is towards the youth and not towards your theological bias, which is quite interesting.

In her account of team dynamics, Hannah makes issues of Christian identity and theology secondary to the impulse of mission. Her distinction between church as a place in which the focus is organizational and theological biases matter, and a mission campus, in which individual and organizational biases need to be negotiated but the priority of mission overrides them, is itself interesting. Eden teams are always a part of a local church and in some situations missional pastoral care can be embedded in the life of a congregation as well as among the team. Hannah's perception of 'church' as a distinct concept from a 'mission campus' also indicates that there may be a way to go before missional congregations become the norm.

Equally, team members do not feel a need to protect their identity from the influence of non-Christians in the community; as Louise put it: 'I've learnt things and I really love them, like [Amy], not like your middle-classy friends but I would enjoy her company more to be honest.' In terms of community activism, Adam's reference above to those with the 'same heart' in his community demonstrates an openness to partnership, a quality that Pears notes as typical of an incarnational approach (2013, p. 104). Such a confident outward orientation is both enabled and underpinned by *missio Dei* theology and by a spirituality defined by the presence of God in daily life. Team members see the good they seek to build on not in terms of what they bring to the community, but rather in identifying the goodness already present in the community. This acknowledges the initiative of God in the world and therefore prioritizes aligning with, and participating in, God's activity, while resisting what is destructive of incoming *shalom*.

Good news-ness

The third theme in an evolving evangelical identity is a new orientation for the missional impulse so central to evangelicalism. Excitement and energy for the good news of Christian faith has been perhaps the greatest gift that evangelicalism has offered to the wider Church. Initially this was focused on communicating the gospel to others and inviting them to conversion, an entirely new practice within sixteenth- and seventeenth-century Protestantism (Bebbington, 1989, pp. 40–1). In time, this momentum also fuelled personal growth and faith development and, in ebbs and flows throughout evangelical history, an engagement in issues of social justice. As Bebbington puts it, evangelicalism inspired 'the dedication that compelled them to act' (1989, p. 71). Missional pastoral care suggests that this missional impulse can change and, for my participants, is changing. Instead of a driven and anxious mission with revival expectations, it is broadening into what I call 'good news-ness', comprised of passion, a lived-out faith, desire for connection and an expectation of God's action.

Passion

Harris describes the nature of contemporary evangelicalism as 'a community of passionate piety', suggesting that while doctrinal priorities are increasingly mixed, the 'experience of a transforming encounter with Christ' remains a unifying factor across the movement (2008, p. 213). This is affirmed by McLaren, who writes: 'When I say I cherish an evangelical identity, I mean something beyond a belief system or doctrinal array or even a practice. I mean an attitude – an attitude towards God and our neighbour and our mission that is passionate' (2006, p. 130). Joy and enthusiasm in response to an encounter with God is a beautiful thing, and a great gift to our communities.

The belief that faith is to be lived out

Following from evangelical passion is the conviction that faith is to impact everyday life, that nominalism is not reflective of the fullness of life offered in Christ. Contemporary evangelicalism retains this sense of vocation in personal lifestyle and moral choices, and in social and political responsibility. Throughout its history, evangelicalism has at times withdrawn from the political and social spheres, but in recent decades involvement in community engagement activities – such as parents and toddler groups, foodbanks and street chaplaincy projects – has become the norm for evangelical congregations (Smith, 2017, p. 28; Thacker, 2010, p. 246). In fact, according to the theologian and mission practitioner Jon Kuhrt, charismatic evangelicals have helped to galvanize the whole Church in social action. While previously different forms of Christianity have remained divided by theological and ethical positions, the recent rise in social action has seen a new willingness to engage beyond silos (2010, p. 14). Charismatic evangelicals have brought their good news-ness to this activity and have worked with others across the Christian tradition, focusing on points of agreement and collaborating in mission.

For participants in the Eden Network, this living out of faith has led to a complete reshaping of lifestyle. In my 2012 article 'Holy Sofas', I quoted a team member who had joined Eden relatively soon after coming to faith themselves. They said:

> It was part of . . . us working out what it meant to be a Christian actually . . . it wasn't just buying into church, it wasn't just buying a ticket to heaven or anything like that but actually we were saved for a reason. (Thompson, 2012, p. 50)

Connection as motivation

A further element of good news-ness found among my participants is the shift from cultural or theological critique to connection with the urban 'other', the person we have previously seen as different. As I have described above, perceiving God at work in urban communities and urban people allows mission practitioners to focus on aligning with that incoming *shalom* rather than protecting or defining their own identity. Instead of the reactive theology and practices adopted throughout the history of evangelicalism, in the development of missional pastoral care as a new practical and theological mode of living the motivation has not been cultural critique but rather the desire for connection. Having moved into a community, admittedly an act that itself embodies a critique of both Church and world, team members were then simply faced with the hope of getting to know people, and in time found ways to connect, share their lives and build community.

Emergent, progressive and post-evangelical groups have often focused on theological deconstruction in the personal journeys of members themselves. Individuals who have found the strictures of modernist evangelicalism painful, even damaging, have needed time and space to process, detox and re-envision their faith. While valid, this is quite a different motivation for theological reflection from that of the missional practitioners I interviewed. The challenges to their inherited theologies arose through their encounter with people who were very different from them – whom they had, in the past, 'othered' – allowing cultural and theological assumptions to colour their attitudes. When they began to call such 'others' friends and neighbours and to find that their assumptions and theologies did not do them justice, they were forced to return to God, to the Bible and to their tradition and ask different questions.

An evangelicalism that can be moved into theological reflection by its missional encounters with those who are different will be continually energized and challenged by the God who is, in Godself, always other!

An expectation that something will happen

The final element of good news-ness is derived from the spirituality of missional pastoral care outlined in the previous chapter: the expectation that something will happen. This expectation is rooted in the belief in God's activity in the world, but modified from the constrictive definitions – of conversion and adoption of middle-class values – so prevalent in modernist evangelicalism. In missional pastoral care the broad hope is for flourishing with its accompanying ambiguity – the complex good that missional pastoral care creates. On a day-to-day basis, this looks like the expectation that glimpses of *shalom* will be seen and experienced in a community: small steps towards a stronger love of self, expressions of agency, more positive life choices, awareness of a good God and mutuality in conversations, time spent together and shared activity. All this is not simply human effort, nor is it passive or aimless. In the usually mundane and the occasionally spectacular, the background thrum is that God is on the move.

Good news-ness offers a way for the evangelical missional impulse to evolve that is rooted in missional practice. Gathering together passion, the belief that faith is to be lived and a fresh motivation seeking connection with those who we may have 'othered' leads to encounters with God in unexpected places and people. Tempering and loosening the expected ways that such encounters might play out enables a gentle constancy, realism and generous attentiveness to the gift of God's withness in everyday life.

A *bigger story*

Recognizing the importance of doctrine within evangelicalism, theological reflection on encountering God in those we have 'othered' offers vital resources for an evolving evangelical identity. In the last two chapters I have drawn out the theological shifts made, to varying degrees, by team and community members. These provide a practical theological paradigm, derived from missional experience: a transition from the 'lost world filled with lost people' to the image of God in every person, and God on God's mission in the world; from an emphasis on the agency of the Church to the recognition of the personhood of all; from a linear 'salvation plan' involving a crisis moment of change from the old to the radically new, to a messy, non-linear process of remaking meaning-systems and leaning into both flourishing and ambiguity; and from heightened expectations of ever-increasing growth to a recognition of limitation, and the slow, incremental nature of human change – the mustard seed of the kingdom.

Engaging this changing narrative with the doctrinal priorities of evangelicalism demonstrates the more expansive theological landscape created by missional pastoral care, which also resonates with others writing about the future theological trajectory of evangelicalism. To begin to shape a theological vision for an evolving evangelical identity, I will revisit the five doctrinal characteristics prioritized by the EA: biblicism, Christocentrism, crucicentrism, conversionism and activism; and, along the way, touch on the ideas of the transformed life, revival expectations and transdenominational networks.

First, what has happened to a commitment to the Bible in the course of mission practice?

Given my comments above regarding changes in epistemology, it may seem that the Bible risks becoming sidelined. In fact, as the use of Scripture among my participants demonstrates, it remains central, but in a way more reminiscent of Stanley Grenz's 'illuminated' text. The Christians I interviewed understood the Bible to be authoritative, in the sense that it is received as the story of origins of the relation between God and humanity. They also read it as a story in which they play an ongoing part, as team member Adam described:

> I love Isaiah 61, you know, 'the Spirit of the sovereign Lord is upon me to preach good news to the poor, bind up the broken hearted and to set the captives free', yeah, I just think that sums everything up. The reason we're here is because God has anointed us, we've got God's anointing, God's authority to go out into the streets to see transformation, to see broken hearts being healed and to see the captives set free . . .

The Bible is seen in missional pastoral care as the framework of an ongoing narrative, fuelled by the Holy Spirit, in which Christians play a part. Mission practitioners continue to return to Scripture when the initial images and passages that framed their mission no longer seem to fit, illustrating their commitment to the Bible and their willingness to wrestle with it as it is 'illuminated' by the Spirit in a particular time and place (Harris, 2008, p. 209).

Second and third, the Evangelical Alliance adopt both christocentrism and crucicentrism, adding a focus on the person of Jesus alongside his salvific work on the cross. This broad focus on the life and death of Jesus resonates with missional pastoral care's incarnational roots in which the whole of Jesus' life, death and resurrection is viewed as a resource for ministry. Team member Louise describes her view of a disciple as: 'somebody who becomes more like Jesus, and to be Christlike, then I would say that has been, is, my journey'. In her desire to imitate Jesus, Louise sets Jesus' death and resurrection in the context of his life and ministry. Team member James echoed this sense of emulating Jesus: 'It's what Christians should be doing anyway, should be engaging with communities and moving to places where actually society's forgotten them, Jesus came for the sinners.' The researcher Andrew Wier argues that evangelical urban ministry needs to be 'informed by a more comprehensive Christological framework', citing David Bosch's concept: 'totus Christus – his incarnation, earthly life, death, resurrection, and parousia' (Bosch, 2011, p. 399; Wier, 2013, p. 109). In this sense then, Christocentrism is evident in missional pastoral care – but what about crucicentrism?

The sole focus on substitutionary atonement in Bebbington's crucicentrism is already set in context by Christocentrism and is further diffused as conversion is set within a framework of broader life change. This tendency to move away from crucicentrism is also evident in Grenz's theology (Harris, 2008, p. 210); Harris concludes that evangelical theologies of atonement are not so much disappearing but expanding, and this affirms the emphasis on flourishing within missional pastoral care. He writes:

There is slowly a shift away from a focus on the cross as a substitutionary act of atonement to appease an offended Deity (or the cross as retributive justice), to an exploration of the cross as a vehicle of restorative justice. Rather than ask if the cross represents a victory over sin, death or the devil, it would seem appropriate for postmodern evangelicals to respond 'all of the above, and more beside . . .' (2008, p. 212).

Fourth, conversionism remains a priority within missional pastoral care, but understandings of the salvation appropriated by conversion have broadened beyond personal belief in Jesus to resemble Bosch's 'comprehensive salvation', which 'is as coherent, broad and deep as the needs and exigencies of human existence' (2011, p. 410). This is reflective of wider shifts within evangelicalism; as Harris notes, evangelical understandings of salvation have become more holistic: 'Instead of salvation from the world, we are also saved for the world, including the poor, the oppressed and the environment' (2008, p. 204). Conversionism in missional pastoral care is largely expressed in terms of missional intent, as team member Dan from Manchester explains:

> It's the parable, Jesus talking about you have to be the light of the world, people have to see you, and it's just like with Eden, it's just being intentional and people seeing you . . . doing things because of God and for God and making them question about stuff.

While Harris perceives a shift from individually orientated evangelism towards an expansive mission among evangelicals (2008, p. 204), missional pastoral care does include faith-sharing. Also, for the team members I interviewed, conversion is still an anticipated outcome – primarily referred to as receiving salvation, or coming to faith in Jesus – and an aspect of the flourishing brought about by missional pastoral care. This can be likened to Warner's addition of the 'transformed life' in his revised quadrilateral (2007, pp. 17–18) and is evident in team members' focus on community building. In missional pastoral care, salvation is understood as encompassing every aspect of life: personal, social and political, while being signified by faith in Jesus:

I supposed the first one has to be getting saved but other things spring to mind things like healings, just realizing that people are loved by God, answered prayer, I wouldn't have said this in the past but I think now community transformation is what we want to see. (Michael)

In moving away from ideas of a linear missional narrative containing moments of conversion followed by radical life change, my participants blur the picture of conversion most commonly presented in contemporary evangelical churches. This is actually not new. As I noted earlier, views on whether conversion is a crisis moment or a process have fluctuated throughout evangelical history (Bebbington, 1989, pp. 7–8). However, it does represent a further shift, again recognized by Harris as a 'greater openness to conversion as a journey . . . [and] a move away from the boundary setting that has characterised evangelicalism, to a greater inclusivity' (2008, p. 205).

Finally, Bebbington's activism, 'the expression of the gospel in effort' (1989, p. 3), is reimagined in missional pastoral care as good news-ness – a passionate commitment to a missional lifestyle that contributes to the hermeneutical process of life change. While the energy and motivation that initiated the relocation of Eden teams is a clear example of activism, in missional pastoral care, effort has been tempered by an understanding of *missio Dei*. This has led to teams acknowledging their secondary role; as Michael states: 'Well everything that matters is done by Him at the end of the day . . . there's no way we could have pulled this stuff off on our own.' This gives activism a different character, less prone to the 'saviour' complex, which can accompany missional efforts (Bosch, 2011, pp. 295–6). It also questions the heightened 'revival expectations' that characterize much of modernist evangelicalism and that were reflected in one team member's initial expectation: 'We thought there would be this, about twelve of us originally, you know the disciples, we're going to come and we're going to transform this whole community' (Thompson, 2012, p. 52). In missional pastoral care, activism remains intentional but is expressed in team members' daily interactions set in the context of God's action in their lives and in the lives of their neighbours and friends. Expectations are orientated towards a complex good, looking for flourishing and welcoming the ambiguity that accompanies it along the way.

Renewing evangelical identity by framing it more positively and identifying what it is we gather around, not just what we stand against, can energize missional activity. The Evangelical Alliance's research suggests that young adults (aged 16–24) are less likely to call themselves evangelical (2011, p. 18), indicating that for the future of the tradition a rethink is necessary. Evangelical theologians such as Tom Greggs are seeking to do this, offering theological reflection that takes seriously the criticisms of evangelicalism (2010, p. 7); and Brian Harris proposes an expansive vision of evangelicalism as missional communities of invitation, welcome and embrace (2008, p. 213).

By owning and embracing its history as a tradition, evangelicalism can revisit its epistemology and reimagine its relationship to cultural context and to the context of the individual. This enables an evangelical affirmation of God in the world and the image of God in human personhood. In so doing we can relax, and instead of defending orthodoxy, evangelicalism can demonstrate a robust faith in the goodness and presence of God and simply align itself with *shalom*, God's kingdom peace, wherever it is evident in the world. Good news-ness characterizes this joining in with God, being people with passion, whose faith shapes daily life, who seek connection and expect something to happen. In this way, evangelicals begin to embody a bigger story by participating in the unfolding narrative of God in the world in what Tom Wright describes as 'faithful improvisation' (2005, pp. 89–92).

Making such changes will require a substantial shift within the networks and organizations that sustain evangelical subculture. Rather than functioning to separate evangelicals from the wider Church and world, organizations need to find ways to facilitate the encounters with those we have 'othered' in order that we might meet with God. And instead of creating identity narratives that ordinary evangelicals are invited to live into, networks could listen closely to the complexity and gift of the experiences of ordinary evangelicals and facilitate a conversation about evangelical identity that is informed by local congregations, mission practitioners and those who don't call themselves Christians, with whom we seek to connect.

Note

1 In my work I often talk to people who are looking for a new model of mission, a new strategy or tactic that will 'work'. While I understand this, if we fail to acknowledge the theological foundations of our practice, changes to our strategies won't stick. We won't see the 'results' we're hoping for and the new tactics will be deemed to have failed. It may not in fact be that they have failed, instead it may be that we didn't go on the theological journey ourselves in order to really inhabit new practices with all of their implications for our own meaning-systems.

7

The View From Here

The incarnational urban mission model of the Eden Network has ended up delivering more than was bargained for. Rather than being an end-point in itself it has opened up a new landscape of missional possibilities and theological trajectories. In my time working for Eden I used to talk about the 'five-year idea'. It often seemed that teams found a distinctive focus for their community involvement after being in their neighbourhood for around five years – maybe a healthcare initiative, a response to local homelessness, alternative education for excluded young people. It took time for team members to settle in and learn to listen, and these new directions often could not have been predicted when the team first moved in. Specific projects arose from the unique combination of the people in the community itself and team members as they became a part of the community and learnt how they might offer their gifts alongside those of the people already there. My point is that you can't see the same view from the foot of the mountain as you can from the top, or from the south side of a lake as from the north. However much we may like to plan and anticipate the path along which mission will take us, ultimately engagement with people you haven't met yet, who are different from you, is a journey into the unknown.

Mission changes everyone involved, meaning that the one thing we do know is that we can't know the destination. We cannot foresee the unique ways that new relationships will add to or take from our lives, or the things that we will create together. I set out on this programme of research, wrestling with what was meant by transformation and feeling unsettled by the sense that reality wasn't fully understood in all its gift and cost. I could not have imagined missional pastoral care at that point, although it was there in the experiences that seemed most significant to me. This is the process of Practical Theology, to give careful and rigorous attention to life experiences (in this case through ethnographic research) and to draw these experiences into conversation with Scripture, theological writing and complementary disciplines such as urban studies or psychology, in order to discern the ways that God is at work and what they may have to say to us.

The incarnational urban mission experiences of team and community members have shown that God is at work in the world, so our theologies of mission need to embrace context, learning from and aligning with *shalom* as we see it in the communities around us. God is also at work in people of all faiths and none, meaning that our theologies of mission need to affirm the *imago Dei* in all people. We have seen that life change happens through a parabolic process of disrupting and reinventing our personal meaning-systems – hermeneutical play – and that we need both a challenge to perspective and the safety of relationships that affirm our personhood in order to enter into the process of change.

Missional pastoral care is a way of life that enables hermeneutical play through its commitment to difference, locality, availability, practicality, long-term consistency and love. The outcomes of missional pastoral care, with its meaning-making processes, are a complex good in the lives of both team and community members – everyone involved experiences flourishing and ambiguity in the course of their relationships. As a model of mission, missional pastoral care presents a challenge to evangelical working theologies. Team members offer insight into evangelical theology and practice from their perspective as volunteer mission practitioners, while the working-class 'recipients' of their – largely middle-class – evangelical mission are able to define it for themselves. As a result, missional pastoral care can offer resources for a twenty-first-century evangelicalism shaped by an awareness of its history, a freedom from self-protection in favour of aligning with incoming *shalom,* and a posture of good news-ness, all of which are held by a bigger theological story.

This research is inevitably a snapshot of experiences from some of those involved with the Eden Network's incarnational urban mission at a particular point in time. The stories of my participants have not ended; their journeys have continued in the non-linear and incremental messiness of missional pastoral care. So I cannot claim to represent the Network as a whole, or as it is right now, or into the future. This research is also limited in its scope, and by its nature as a qualitative, ethnographic study, and has been undeniably shaped by my standpoint and approach. Another researcher may have approached the topic very differently; there is more to be said about youth work as the first priority for Eden teams, and about the role of, and implications for, Eden's partner churches in this model of missional living. Missional pastoral care is my own language, a concept that for me expresses the collective experiences of team and community members who participated in the study. It is also an emergent and tentative form of ministry, with team members still grappling with the influence of their inherited theological narratives. Nevertheless, despite its limitations, as the ideas presented here resonate with the experiences of Christians in mission and the people they come alongside, they can provide insight and raise important questions, encouraging others to reflect on their own practical theological journey.

Taking in all that has been learnt from the experiences of mission practitioners and so-called 'recipients' of their mission in urban communities, the view from here has implications for existing mission models and for pastoral care. It also suggests approaches for mission practitioners, leaders and congregations wanting to engage or engage more deeply with their communities. Furthermore, by seeing evangelicalism as a tradition in the light of this research, its gift to the Church and wider society comes into sharper focus. In this final chapter I explore these implications and offer some ways forward for future mission.

Implications for models of mission

Reflecting on some common mission models in the light of missional pastoral care, with its particular view of God and of the missional task, it is evident that there are points of overlap and of difference. Here, I briefly want to draw some comparisons with personal witnessing, evangelistic events, exploring Christianity courses and social action projects as models for congregational mission, and make some suggestions for the role of pastoral care within mission. Missional pastoral care, and the research that sits behind it, brings a new perspective to these themes – highlighting what it is about models of mission that make them effective and, equally, why some of them might not be as effective as many would hope.

Witnessing to friends and family

By 'witnessing' I mean the small-scale, everyday, hoped-for conversations about faith with people we already know, such as work colleagues, friends and family members. In many evangelical churches, being encouraged to seek out opportunities to witness is a regular occurrence and intended to underpin other mission models such as events or courses. While it may appear to have the most in common with missional pastoral care, witnessing is often perceived to be a special category of conversation, and one that generates anxiety for many Christians. How does witnessing differ from simply talking about our lives with others, sharing stories and priorities, being honest about what is going on and what is important for us?

Efforts to help Christians to feel comfortable talking about their faith lead to exercises such as practising telling your testimony or using diagrams to explain the gospel story. While these may have some merit, they introduce a formality to faith-talk and imply that there is a right and a wrong way to do it, thereby removing the natural sharing of ourselves in relationship that might otherwise help us talk about our faith more easily. As a special category of conversation, witnessing risks becoming a mini-sermon, with the Christian doing all the talking. In this scenario it is clear that a response is expected, and that the Christian hopes it will be a positive one. This sets up an unequal exchange as the assumption is that the Christian is there to communicate a message that they believe to be true, regardless of what the listener thinks about it.

While many Christians feel extremely vulnerable sharing their faith, we can often be oblivious to the vulnerability that the listener experiences. Knowing that their friend or family member is putting themselves out there, and knowing that a positive response is desired, places considerable pressure on the listener, who may profoundly disagree with what is shared, may not have thought much about faith before, or may not have been prepared to have a conversation about their spiritual beliefs that day. These interactions can feel one-sided rather than mutual and so cease to be a conversation at all; especially when it involves someone we care about, we are acutely aware of how awkward this kind of encounter can be.

Such a formal approach to faith-talk also jars with the processes of life change I have observed in this research. Missional pastoral care indicates that people change as they re-evaluate their meaning-systems, enabled by a challenge to perspective alongside an affirmation of personhood. Witnessing constitutes a strong challenge to perspective, but due to its one-sided approach, loaded with expectations about who is right and who is wrong, it often fails to respect and affirm the personhood of the listener, leading to the conversation being perceived as threatening or judgemental, with the inevitable defensive response.

Missional pastoral care is different both in its motivation and approach. Among my research participants, talking about faith was not a special category of conversation to be practised and geared up for. Conversations about faith came about through curiosity, getting to know one another, and finding out about one another's lifestyles. In this respect, faith-sharing is another facet of availability, the willingness to be open about your life in ways that include your faith. It also differs from witnessing in that the expected response is simply for the other person to also share their life story. Witnessing is often perceived as a form of persuasion, the aim being to convince the other person that you are right about the subject. In missional pastoral care, faith-sharing is not intended to persuade or demand a response. Sharing your life narrative is an open offering of yourself in relationship, not laden with unspoken expectations.

Mutuality in missional pastoral care means that team members not only shared their stories of life and faith, but they also listened to the experiences of others, learning not to assume that someone had no faith because they expressed it differently from them. Faith-sharing becomes less intimidating when an equal part of the task is to listen to how the other person feels about God and the world, their beliefs and experiences of faith so far. This kind of listening has enabled the Christians among my research participants to learn to hear from God or to see something of God in or through someone else's story. To receive the gift of revelation through someone else, and to let them know that they just showed you something of God, is a powerful expression of faith in itself.

So missional pastoral care includes conversation about faith, but the underlying convictions, motivations and context make it quite different from witnessing as it is understood by many Christians. Holding these two models of conversation about faith side by side, faith-sharing in missional pastoral care seems to hold more promise for enabling life change and for helping people to embrace Christian faith, as it is more attuned to the ways change actually happens. This, then, presents a challenge in how we encourage people to talk about faith in our churches. Naming some of the difficulties presented by witnessing may help to open up a conversation about healthier and more mutual ways to share our life and faith stories with others, such that we all may grow through the process.

Events evangelism

From large-scale events with popular evangelists, to Christian concerts, smaller regional and local 'seeker-friendly' social events, meals or church services, churches and Christian organizations offer a range of events intentionally designed to appeal to not-yet-Christians. These are often used to give local Christians a focus in their personal witnessing, an accessible and credible event to invite along a friend or family member. The event then takes responsibility for presenting the Christian message clearly and relevantly, often with an invitation to respond to the message in some way, allowing the Christian or local church to follow up in conversation with individuals. Evangelical Christianity has a long tradition of events evangelism, most famously the mass evangelistic rallies of Billy Graham and others from the 1950s and throughout the last half of the twentieth century.

This approach to mission has perhaps the least in common with missional pastoral care. An event is just a moment in time and therefore can only be a small, if significant, part of the longer story of a person's journey of faith. However, in our narratives of mission we often fail to articulate this longer journey. Partly perhaps through a desire for succinct story-telling, partly through a wish that life be simpler than it actually is, our talk about mission often gives the impression that coming to an event and making a 'decision' is the sum total of becoming a Christian. In Chapter 4, I described this as the 'view from the stage'.

Much of the narrative of evangelical mission has been shaped by its key leaders, within a leadership culture that values charisma and authoritarianism. From the stage, the numbers of people attending and subsequent numbers of people responding to the message constitutes the outcome, or impact, of the event. What is missing in many evangelical leaders' understanding of mission is the view from the street. It is the ordinary Christian who, having invited their colleague or friend, then continues the relationship after such an event, but who is often not offered ways to navigate that ongoing story, which might not fit a 'testimony' narrative. As a result of this skewed perspective, evangelistic events can often be perceived to be far more effective than they actually are, and therefore can be seen as a panacea for churches longing to see growth (Guest, 2007,

p. 25). Bigger is assumed to be better, and professionalized events management is seen as the solution to offering a relevant Christian message.

Missional pastoral care offers a different lens with which to understand the dynamics at work in events-based mission. Evangelistic events offer a degree of challenge to perspective – they might open the eyes of a person not familiar with church to the fact that Christianity still has a crowd of followers, that churches might use contemporary music, and that sermons can be funny and thought-provoking and not just soporific. These are good things. Such events also usually include a clear invitation to respond, or at least raise the question of how one might respond to the Christian message. This can catalyse a person's thinking, bringing to awareness what may have been rumbling along under the surface for some time.

So an event could play a positive role in providing that challenge to perspective which is essential for a change in meaning-system. But it misses some vital elements that missional pastoral care has shown are necessary for life change: an affirmation of personhood, repetition, consistency and practice. Obviously, events are only a drop in the ocean of a person's life experience. Missional pastoral care demonstrates that repeated bumping into the Christian message in different forms and to different degrees provides the opportunity for gradual reflection and re-evaluation of personal meaning-systems. This suggests a partial role for events within the context of a missional relationship.

But evangelistic events can also be shaped by the evangelical missional narrative in ways that may be unhelpful. The aim of many, if not all, evangelistic events is to offer the attendee a taste of what they are missing – to show how great, technicolour and fantastic being a Christian is, compared to how empty or meaningless not being a Christian is. This exemplifies the polarization of the lost world and the Church in the evangelical missional narrative, and undermines rather than affirms personhood, suggesting that who you are right now is not good enough, but by becoming 'one of us' you could become better. Alongside this the presentational nature of many events doesn't give space for the agency and contribution of people exploring faith; attendees are passive, and voices from the stage are seen as authoritative. This doesn't create mutuality, invite participation or give opportunity to practise alternative meanings, features of missional pastoral care that help people move towards life change.

It is easy to fall into a professionalized model of event delivery; many churches describe this as seeking 'excellence' and as treating the people who come as 'honoured guests'. While this is well intentioned, it presents two specific challenges. First, it buys into the individualism and consumerism of Western middle-class culture. Second, and relatedly, it perpetuates the separation between 'us' and 'them', as the host performs for their guests, demonstrating their skills and resources, rather than truly encountering them person to person.

The recognition of power dynamics and systemic injustice within missional pastoral care challenges models that reduce people to consumers and shows that overcoming the 'us' and 'them' is actually the primary task in mission. An 'excellent' event may impress attendees and, if it echoes their cultural values, they may well continue to attend; but this approach risks people adopting the role of consumer, rather than participant, in the body of Christ. The challenge to perspective then becomes entirely personal and internal – about the state of your heart, not about the *shalom* that God invites the world to enter into. For people struggling against poverty, or seeking a place to belong in the midst of their vulnerability, 'excellence' can be impressive but exclusive, as people simply do not see themselves reflected in such a polished presentation of Christian life. Finding belonging is about being seen, heard and accepted for who we are. This requires a different kind of event in which people come to recognize their own significance as they contribute and participate in community life.

Evangelistic events have limited potential in contributing to a change in someone's meaning-system. They may play a part, causing a long-term, relational process to come to conscious awareness, and creating a moment of decision that can catalyse or confirm a change in meaning-system. However, how an event is designed is important: does it affirm the personhood of those who attend, or does it encourage an 'all bad' to 'all good' narrative of conversion? Does it objectify attendees, requiring them to passively receive an authoritarian presentation from the stage, or are multiple perspectives valued and each person a participant? And does it, in its delivery and in its content, do justice to the full Christian message – which is good news to *all* people and to our planet? The learning from missional pastoral care may help to shape events carefully and to acknowledge the limited role they can play in processes of life change, so that we can use them appropriately without unrealistic expectations for them to fulfil all of our aspirations for mission.

Exploring Christianity courses

Missional course programmes are a popular way for churches to help their congregations reach out to friends and family. Broadly, they involve a group format with elements of hospitality, formal presentation and discussion, delivered over a number of sessions. This model has more potential for affirming the personhood of participants in that it aligns with some of the key features of missional pastoral care: recognizing conversion as a process and prioritizing relational and experiential styles of learning.

By including discussion and creating a culture that is more exploratory than focused on conversion decisions, missional courses acknowledge that people attending have something to bring to the conversation and give space for their views to be heard. Importantly, they allow for conversion to be an incremental process, albeit often signified by a moment of commitment, throughout the sessions. A course might be seen as a microcosm of the open-ended and community-based relationships of missional pastoral care, with the content taking participants on a journey of gathering information, getting to know and trust one another and shaping one another's understanding. So the significance of a course is rooted in the group's relationships, which involve sharing ideas and experiences.

The sharing of life and life stories in both words and through doing things together that happens in missional pastoral care can also be a strength of a group going through a course, who may meet in one another's homes and eat together as part of the experience.

Exploring Christianity courses are acknowledged to have been more successful in helping people to find and continue in Christian faith than large-scale events (Guest, 2007, pp. 45–6; Warner, 2007, pp. 118–9). I would suggest that this is due to the way that this model provides a degree of affirmation of personhood, through its relational and conversational style, alongside a challenge to perspective. By creating a process of shared experiences and reflection over time, these courses offer a way into Christian faith that is more consistent with the processes of hermeneutical play that lead to life change. But missional pastoral care demonstrates the importance of attention to context and leaving room for the unexpected to emerge within missional encounters. The production of exploring Christianity courses as resources has meant that they have been easily delivered in varied settings across the country. While some see this breadth as a strength, it can also be seen as marketing a particular perspective on Christian faith without attention to the context and perspectives of those receiving the materials (Hunt, 2005, p. 76).

As with evangelistic events, much depends on *how* the course materials are used locally as to whether they are the starting point for a conversation or seen as the authoritative voice in the room. A formal presentational style could limit the degree to which participants feel their personhood is affirmed and, combined with standardized materials that make no reference to the particular situations of participants' lives, may mean that the course experience is more about 'fitting in' to a Christian culture than finding God within your own. Missional pastoral care's commitment to locality challenges this 'one size fits all' approach. In missional pastoral care, Christian faith, in all its imperfect reality, is lived out in relationship with another person and, over time, stories of life and faith are shared and patterns of living are shaped by one another, overcoming the disconnect between a person's local context, life experience and Christian faith.

Social action projects

As we have seen, in recent decades the changing nature of poverty in our society means that most churches are now in close proximity to people experiencing some form of marginalization. In Chapter 3, I explored the difference between needs-based 'charity' and strengths-based approaches to poverty that promote the personhood of people struggling against poverty and give space for them to exercise agency in shaping their lives and communities. Widespread engagement in social action projects has drawn evangelical churches into a highly politicized public space, including food poverty, Universal Credit sanctions and homelessness. The charity model is dominant within UK culture, and this is reflected within church social action as most projects take a needs-based approach, either offering a service (such as a free meal or food parcels) or advocacy (such as filling in forms on behalf of people or campaigning for marginalized groups).

While evangelicals, influenced by the evangelical missional narrative, have primarily viewed poverty in individualized terms and often understood social action as a precursor to evangelism (Smith, 2017, p. 32), their involvement has led to encounters with those they may have previously 'othered'. This is far more diffuse and less immersive than the experiences of the mission practitioners in missional pastoral care. However, there are similar dynamics at play: meeting people who are very different from you and the desire to build a connection with them. Evangelicals, along with other Christians engaging in social action, often bump into some common issues. Their foodbank, community meal or homeless ministry may not result in as many people becoming part of the church congregation as they had hoped. They may have a suspicion that while it is good to meet people's immediate needs, resources are tight, demand is growing, and there is no long-term solution to the larger social, political and economic issues that brought them to the project in the first place. Also, the people using their services may simply seem dependent or stuck, not 'able' to make choices to improve their situation.

These questions lead some into political activism, some into praying for God's miraculous intervention, and some into weariness. The question that motivated this research – 'What does it take to change a life?' – is felt keenly by many volunteering faithfully in church community projects. The result of such experiences is an interest among some evangelical congregations in moving from models of charity towards strengths-based community development.

Missional pastoral care highlights the significance of personhood and offers a theological rationale for strengths-based social action. What the incarnational mission team members and urban community members in my research learnt in one setting, those practising strengths-based community engagement are learning in another: that God is at work in the world; that God's image is in every person, gifting them with presence, creativity and skills to share; and that people flourish when their personhood is affirmed and when they are given the opportunity to begin to imagine their lives differently. It may be a slow and messy process with loss and limitation built in, but the gradual change in meaning-systems does lead to flourishing in all the ways I have described, including a greater awareness of a good God.

To return to Sam Wells's four responses to poverty, missional pastoral care is an example of both being and working with, but also goes beyond Wells's ideas, as in the process of missional pastoral care, the 'with' collapses. In missional pastoral care the 'them' and 'us' becomes simply 'we', 'us together here': in the desire for all to see and experience *shalom* in community; and in the sense that God's mission is to both team members and urban community members as everyone participates in hermeneutical play, leading to flourishing and ambiguity. This creates a network of relationships that is messy and uneven but within which each person is being changed.

Pastoral care as mission

Within my evaluation of each of the models outlined above, hermeneutical play – the process of challenging and changing meaning-systems through relationships – is paramount. That this is a concept more commonly recognized within pastoral counselling indicates that perhaps the separation of mission and pastoral care in the Christian lexicon is unhelpful, masking what is really going on. Missional pastoral care demonstrates that pastoral care, as hermeneutical play, is integral to the mission of God, and this has some implications for pastoral care.

Pastoral care can be seen as overly 'problem-centred' in that it is dominated by a therapeutic model of ministry (Stoddart, 2012, pp. 331–2). Focusing solely on 'problems' means that it is less suited to helping people who are concerned simply with personal growth and self-development, a common feature of twenty-first-century Western society. Through its emphasis on meaning-making and everyday mutuality, missional pastoral care is a different form of caring, one that is able to respond to aspirations of personal growth as well as specific problems.

As a community-based model requiring a wide network of relationships, missional pastoral care also prevents pastoral care from remaining individualistic, or from neglecting the wider picture of social, political and cultural forces that impact a person's life. It repositions pastoral care as a form of Christian ministry in contemporary society, moving away from a professionalized, counselling-orientated and church-based service for Christians to something much more foundational to the life and mission of the community of faith and its relationship to the world. Missional pastoral care doesn't replace the need for professional pastoral counsellors. It does recognize, however, that while expertise may be needed occasionally, there is an important role for ordinary people in establishing regular and mutual relationships of care in which there is affirmation, trust and challenge and in which the ongoing task of meaning-making can be worked out in daily life.

Finally, by integrating faith-sharing with pastoral care in relationships of parabolic meaning-making, missional pastoral care takes pastoral care beyond 'needs-meeting', and prevents it from being used simply as a means to the end of evangelism. Instead, the separation of mission and pastoral care is overcome and pastoral care, as meaning-making, is shown to be the very substance of God's activity, God's mission, in both the Christian and the non-Christian.

Practising missional pastoral care

There have been many great books written on mission, and while we might like the idea of a well-tested model that can be learnt and implemented in any community, I'm not sure such a thing really exists. Taking seriously the activity of God in communities and the need for mutuality in missional relationships means that we can't begin with a pre-defined model. Instead, tools, resources and encouragement are needed to allow missional approaches to emerge in our own contexts. Missional pastoral care is not a franchise, or 'mission-in-a-box' that you can roll out locally. It is an approach that offers some guideposts for the journey of genuinely contextual mission: that which arises from within a particular place or situation.

There are a number of ways in which I hope this material can be of benefit to those engaged in mission – whether church leaders, community workers, congregations or mission team members. It may help you to be aware of what you bring to the task of mission and to understand the dynamics of how people change. It might also help to get started or to change direction, and to set realistic expectations for the outcomes of your missional activity. Ultimately, it can remind you to remain open to what unexpected gifts might be created as you and others in your community – along with God – begin to discover *shalom* together.

Whatever your situation, none of us comes to the idea of mission with a clean slate. Even if you have never been involved in mission before, your ideas about what it is, the activity you have seen and heard about, the sermons you have heard preached, will all shape your new practices. One way you might use this research is to reflect on your own personal meaning-system and your inherited missional narratives. Try

---

Reflecting on inherited narratives

Spend some time thinking about the shaping influences and significant moments of your life in relation to mission. What Bible passages, themes or theological ideas speak to you about mission? For example, you might choose the parable of the Good Samaritan, or the Apostle Paul's theme of becoming 'all things to all people'. Write them down and share them together if you are working as a group.

Ask yourself, what kind of story do these ideas tell?

What is the world of the story like?
Who are the main characters in the story?
What is the action or plot of the story?
What genre is the story? Is it a comedy, a thriller or an arthouse cinema experience?

Think about, or discuss in your group, the implications of your stories for your mission. Do they affirm the personhood of all people? Do they offer a challenge to perspective? Do they give space for mission, leading to loss and ambiguity as well as flourishing? You might like to refer to the evangelical missional narrative and the spirituality of missional pastoral care, with its alternative theological lenses as discussed in Chapter 5. Give yourself some space and time to grapple with these ideas with others and in prayer. See how God might help you understand your story as part of your journey in your own particular time and place.

How might that change the way you engage in mission?

the following exercise, either on your own or with a group or team.

It's likely that, having been interested enough to pick this book up and make it to the end, you are already, or have been, involved in mission activity to some extent. Perhaps you lead, or work for, a church or mission organization. You will no doubt be very familiar with the mission models discussed earlier in this chapter. If witnessing, evangelistic events or exploring Christianity courses are your current default approach to mission, missional pastoral care invites you to ask some different questions. You might take a look at your existing mission activity and consider *how* you go about it. Could you adapt your approach to more strongly affirm personhood, involving people not just as passive attendees but as participants? Or might you acknowledge the time it takes for real meaning-system change, factoring this into your expectations and planning? In addition, reflect on the daily lives of your congregation members aside from those distinct models of mission; how do they relate to the dynamics of difference, locality, availability, practicality, long-term consistency and love? You might find some people in your congregation who already live in this way in their neighbourhoods and who might be able to encourage others to live missionally where they are.

It may be that you are involved in Christian social action, and while you recognize some of the dynamics of missional pastoral care that I have described, your activity tends to be needs-based in its approach. You may be wondering how you might move to a strengths-based way of doing things in order to create the mutuality and flourishing seen in missional pastoral care. Changing a culture that is already established will take time and intentional action from all involved. But there are steps that you can take. First, begin to have the conversation with your team, colleagues or congregation. Share these ideas with them, preach about *shalom, missio Dei* and the image of God in all people. Draw out the theological missional narratives that are at play in your context and consider how they might need to change.

As a team, begin to discuss together what gifts you notice in the people who engage with your mission. Look out for times when people who don't describe themselves as Christians remind you a little of Jesus. Think together about how you might change the way that your initiative works on a daily basis. How could you make decisions about the project in ways that include everybody involved? How might you respect and affirm the personhood of people who engage with your activities, giving space for them to play their part and bring their skills? For example, if you volunteer at a foodbank, could you enable people who receive food parcels to also volunteer? Could you create a supermarket-style environment where they are able to choose the foods they like rather than receive a standard food parcel? Alongside enabling people to exercise their agency in your initiative, consider your language; 'service users' or 'clients' is formal and passive – identifying people only by their needs – it is not the language of mutual relationship. Could you begin to refer to everybody as participants? Subtle changes in language can have a huge impact over time. You might even decide that rather than simply providing emergency food, you want to build community through sharing food, and so start a community meal in which everyone cooks and eats together.

Some reading around strengths-based approaches to mission and social action will help you as you continue to reflect. There are suggestions in the Further Reading section, but a good and accessible place to start would be *Fullness of Life Together* and *Building Kingdom Communities*, two reports that I have been involved in writing in partnership with Church Urban Fund (available to download online).

If you have recently begun, or are soon to begin, a new season of life or missional adventure, perhaps even moving into a new community, why not consider shaping your life using missional pastoral care as inspiration? Think about how the seven elements – difference, locality, availability, practicality, long-term commitment, consistency and love – might play out in your new situation. How can you be attuned to the imbalances of power present in your particular context? Rather than having predetermined ideas about how your mission will develop, seek to build mutual relationships and listen to the stories of those who are different from you while also sharing your own. Focus on discerning and aligning with the signs of *shalom* in people and in your community and resisting whatever is destructive of it, and see what happens. I'm confident that God will guide and sustain you and that beautiful new insights and missional initiatives will emerge as you participate in community life along with others.

Wherever you are at in your journey of mission, I hope that missional pastoral care can be an encouragement that if it is slow, messy and painful, all is not lost. Countering our cultural 'success' narratives is a significant challenge and it is important that we find our own language to express what we consider to be a 'win' in our mission. Recognizing that loss and ambiguity are essential parts of the complex good of life change is a step in that direction. Understanding that what feels painful is a part of the process of changing our meaning-systems helps us to persevere and stay present in the discomfort rather than be ground down by feelings of failure or self-criticism. Hold your nerve – God is at work!

Missional pastoral care also makes the case that cultivating personhood in ourselves and others by laying down our belief in our own superiority, and giving space for people to exercise agency and share their gifts, is the path to human flourishing. Seeing people grow in their love of self, begin to make more intentional and positive life choices, becoming increasingly aware of God's good presence in their lives and doing that in mutuality, is such a gift. Crafting mission practices that prioritize personhood means regularly asking ourselves the difficult questions: Whose voice is not being listened to in this situation? Where does power and privilege lie in this group? How can I cheer on someone else rather than do things for them? Why am I tempted to retain control in this situation? Allowing the process of hermeneutical play to be mutual will mean that at times you will experience the ambiguity of the complex good. But it also means that you discover the freedom of not having to be the expert, able to simply bring yourself without superiority and see what can be achieved through the combined gifts of a group or community.

Perhaps the kind of lifestyle I have described as missional pastoral care resonates with you deeply; you may have lived this yourself for a number of years and have had your own questions about whether it counted as mission. I have really been on this journey for you. If you resonate with the feelings of confusion, frustration or failure articulated by team members and need to process some of the loss and ambiguity caused by your mission, I pray that missional pastoral care, by offering language and a framework for your experiences, helps you find ways to do that. You *are* enough and God is with you.

Uncertainty about our own mission and vocation can be painful, but feeling misunderstood by the churches and organizations who oversee us adds a further layer of challenge. By naming the difficulties of 'transformation' language, and conceptualizing missional pastoral care as an emergent evangelical form of missional living, I hope to equip you to see your mission with more clarity and understand the processes of change you are participating in in your community, enabling you to share what you do with greater confidence in your church and organizational settings. In conversations about vision setting and impact measurement, allow the different kinds of outcomes created by missional pastoral care to shape your plans; while it might not yield the results that others expect, this ministry does contribute to God's incoming *shalom*.

It might seem that missional pastoral care is too demanding to be practical as a model of mission; it involves exposure to the vulnerability of meaning-system change, being available to new relationships and maintaining the long-term commitment required. I can understand the appeal of models that are less immersive, and promise quicker, more obvious results. Here I have tried to show what the reality of mission looks like, beyond the rhetoric. It is messy, and long term, and asks us to be open to discomfort and change in ourselves – not just in those we seek to come alongside. This is an honest take on community-based mission that involves pitfalls, risks and hard lessons to learn, as well as gifts and a revelation of God's kingdom. By offering it in its mixedness, I hope it can be of help to you as you venture further in your mission. However you use this research, you will generate your own stories to tell, and I'd love to hear them.

In the last few decades evangelicalism, albeit of varying kinds, has come to be a dominant voice in mainstream British Christianity. Alongside this, mission is increasingly viewed as a fundamental shaping principle for the life of the Church both locally and nationally. Therefore, the way in which mission practice interacts with evangelicalism as a tradition is hugely important. As a result of the current widespread involvement of evangelicals in social activism, the British evangelical sub-culture has an opportunity to begin to listen to those immersed in missional relationships and draw out their questions and concerns; to revisit some of its 'working theologies' and to explore ways that it might cultivate encounters with those we have previously 'othered'.

Such a move would acknowledge that contemporary evangelicalism is a product of, as well as a contributor to, this particular time and place. It could take the tradition from prioritizing the protection of evangelical identity to aligning with God's incoming *shalom* in the world and thriving in its characteristic good news-ness, informed by a bigger theological story. While some might fear that this would lessen evangelical distinctiveness, it is my belief that it would build on the gift of energy and passion that evangelicalism has offered to the Church throughout its history, while rightly acknowledging the need for growth and change: accepting that evangelicals are the focus of God's mission just as much as those who may not call themselves Christians. As individuals and as a tradition, evangelicalism can continue to seek its own 'transformation' by remaining open to the revelation of God in and through missional experience.

Missional pastoral care has much in common with ideas of whole-life discipleship, and therefore might be easily dismissed as nothing new. But we often miss from our talk about whole-life discipleship the necessity of engagement with people who are 'not like us'. Missional pastoral care is fundamentally about sharing life, and life stories, with people who are different, so that we all might change. One of the most significant things you could do in response to this book is to seek to build a mutual, genuine friendship with someone who is very different from you. But this is where many Christians struggle, as our worlds become busy – perhaps filled with church activities – and our culture makes it easy to stick within our tribes so that we have few opportunities to build long-term, mutual friendships with people who are genuinely different from us. A challenge from missional pastoral care is the simplicity of team member Dan's words in Chapter 3 about being available: 'It['s] just a very simple thing I've spent a lot of time doing it, so other people would've done other things but I just did that . . . you decide what you want to invest in don't you, your priorities in your life, and that was one of them.'

A commitment to being in relationship with those who we once considered 'other' brings an important corrective to predominantly middle-class mission. *Missio Dei* theology has been accused of leading to an affirmation of cultural trends that are not ultimately of God. This note of caution is helpful, especially given the dominance of middle-class, Western culture within British Christianity. In suburban congregations made up largely of middle-class professionals, it could be easy to extend the *missio Dei* to baptize the actions of the organizations and structures in which they play a part. In order to retain both the alignment with God's incoming *shalom* and resistance of that which is destructive of that kingdom, it is vital that the voices of those experiencing the brokenness and injustice of social structures are heard within middle-class Christianity, including evangelicalism.

Missional pastoral care is mission shaped from the ground up; the models and theologies of mission organizations and denominational hierarchies are being remade through a creative interaction between ordinary mission practitioners, urban community members and God at work. So often the 'recipients' of mission are invisible in the process of defining it. This research draws attention to their agency in processes of mission, highlighted by the experiences of long-term mission practitioners who discovered not only agency but also a revelation of God in those around them. In large and small ways, in confident and sometimes tentative ways, the 'recipients' of mission become the missioners of the Christians who have sought to come alongside them.

This shift – from mission owned and disseminated by Christian hierarchies to mission emerging among mixed groups of people seeking *shalom* in their worlds – is much needed in order for the Church to flourish into the future. A part of that flourishing is to recognize that as Christians we need revelation of God from those we have perceived as 'other'. Discipleship is to grow to know God more deeply and see God's image more clearly in every human being, especially those whom we might least expect (or want) to bless us. The journeys of team and community members in missional pastoral care show that we are all the focus of God's mission.

I offer this research as a learner not as an expert, in the hope that it is a helpful contribution to the ongoing conversation about mission and marginality. While aware of its limitations, I believe missional pastoral care to be a faithful representation of the experiences of team and urban community members, in which meaning-making has been found to be at the centre of the mission of God, leading to an evolution in evangelical identity and theology. As team members have remained courageously open to God's unexpected work in their mission, and community members have found new ways to flourish in community, in their relationships with one another they demonstrate the mission of God to all people, building mutual communities of care, a foretaste of God's incoming *shalom*.

Appendix:
Practical Theological Research

My intention in this research, and now with this book, has been to see afresh the incarnational urban ministry of the Eden Network. In this sense, the research sits alongside that of sociologists such as Mathew Guest, Anna Strhan, Christian Smith and James Bielo in that it seeks to look between doctrinal statements and subcultural narratives and understand what ordinary evangelicals do with the theologies they inherit – their lived experience. I sought to ask what 'effectiveness' meant in this context and to identify the kinds of ministry practices that were effective in urban communities. In order to do this I developed a research methodology that helped me take off my blinkers and assumptions, and that could enable realistic and robust conclusions. By adopting established methodologies and practising the craft of research with care and integrity, it is possible to produce unforeseen outcomes, genuinely seeing with fresh eyes. Here I share a little more of what I mean by a practical theological approach and the research methodology and methods that it generates, in the hope that it illuminates the process and outcomes of this project.

Practical Theology is a relatively new academic discipline that has developed since the 1970s out of Pastoral Theology. It aspires to take seriously the faith lives of ordinary people within theological research and knowledge. Traditionally, theology has been studied in two broad forms: Systematic Theology, which seeks to categorize and deepen our understanding of doctrine through the study of earlier theologians and religious texts; and applied (or Pastoral) Theology, which takes the work of systematic theologians and applies it to real-life situations. It's the classic sermon structure: begin with the biblical text or a statement of doctrine, discuss what it means, then ask: 'What are the implications of this for us today?'

Practical Theology is different in that it is rooted in the belief that any knowledge of the divine is derived from human experience. The practical theologian Terry Veling describes it as 'more "verb-like" than "noun-like"'. It resists definition because it is 'not a "thing"' as such; rather, it is the recognition that theory and practice are always intertwined and 'it is only in the practice or doing of theology that we begin to realise and understand its meanings and workings more deeply' (2005, p. 4). So Practical Theology takes lived experience as its starting point. This includes experiences of reading sacred texts, prayer and participation in personal and communal religious practices, but is not restricted to such obviously 'religious' types of experience.

This approach to learning resonates with my charismatic Christian formation. I believe that God is with me and that my Christian life is a process of learning and growth into a fuller realization of God's love in the world. In that process God uses all sorts of things to teach me if I take the time to notice: the Bible, other people, TV programmes, books, art, the natural world. Practical Theology for me describes my own spiritual practice, learning more of who God is by paying attention to the world around me and bringing what I see to my theological reflection.

However, ordinary human experience is not always welcomed as a source of knowledge in research. Traditional 'scientific' inquiry uses 'methods of quantitative analysis that are rooted in presumptions of objectivity and large generalizable findings – resulting in irrefutable, conclusive "hard" evidence'. Such an approach prioritizes rational thought over affective insight, and claims to generate universal facts 'that hold true in concrete situations across time and space and thus can be applied in specific contexts and hold universally' (Scharen and Vigen, 2011, pp. 4–5). In some cases and for some research questions, quantitative approaches in controlled environments are entirely appropriate. Nevertheless, every experiment is designed and written up by a person, who will inevitably bring their life experiences to bear on the design and when interpreting the results. It is not possible for research to be completely 'objective', and so it is important to name and account for the perspectives that researchers bring to their projects.

To recognize the validity of experience as a source for theological insight, we also have to consider how we as humans process and then communicate our experiences. Practical Theology finds common ground with qualitative approaches to research through its commitment to lived experience. As such, it takes a constructivist approach to knowledge, or epistemology. This means that it recognizes that humans interpret reality in order to make sense of it; we 'make meaning' from our experiences.

The practical theologians and researchers John Swinton and Hilary Mowat, writing from a Christian perspective, suggest then that 'Reality is real and in principle accessible', but that humans construct 'maps of reality', making meaning through their interpretations. Therefore, rather than simply attending to what people do, it is also necessary to take into account their *understandings* of their own actions and events – the meanings they attach to them within the context of a whole life (2006, pp. 37–8). Practical Theology often involves the study of faith using qualitative methods, the data from which is used 'in the cultivation of theologically-grounded practical wisdom' (Graham, 2013, p. 178).

The aim of Practical Theology is to bring about change in the real lives of the theologian and of those who participate in the situations they research. As a result of its commitment to lived experience as a source for theology and the desire for practical theological learning to change situations in the world, Practical Theology has the potential to be liberative, focusing on giving space for the voices and experiences of those who are not traditionally seen or heard within theology or other fields of research to speak their own words and share their 'practical wisdom'. As Veling writes: 'Practical theology shows a preference for the stranger in our midst, for the neighbour who is close to us, for the one who pleads for mercy or who cries out for justice' (2005, p. 10).

In order to access the real, lived experiences of ordinary people, Practical Theology often adopts ethnographic methods. Ethnography is an approach to qualitative research that literally means 'writing culture', and involves observation and finding ways to hear people's stories – the narratives that contain the meanings they have attributed to their experiences. It originates within anthropology and shares the constructivist epistemological foundations of the wider field of qualitative research and of Practical Theology. Ethnography is often done using a combination of qualitative research methods; at its heart is the desire to understand a particular aspect of human experience from the perspective of those who hold that experience. This understanding is then brought into conversation with wider theories relevant to the research topic.

Ethnography offers a rigorous methodological framework that makes listening to people's stories a robust contribution to academic and theological knowledge. Central to this framework is self-awareness on the part of the researcher. This is called 'reflexivity', meaning to take account of the impact of the researcher on the research process and its outcomes (Hufford, 1999, p. 297). Being reflexive in this project meant giving attention to my own standpoint in relation to the research. As an employee of The Message Trust and part of the national Eden Network team, I was an insider to the Eden Network; and, as a resident in an Eden community and a member of an Eden partner church (although never part of an Eden team), I had experienced some of the complexities of being an incomer into an urban community. I was therefore a 'practitioner-researcher' researching within my own organization and networks (Fox et al., 2007, pp. 76–9; McNiff, 2000).

This particular position brought both gifts and challenges to the research. It enabled me to cultivate what the anthropologist Clifford Geertz describes as both 'experience-near' and 'experience-distant' perspectives. Geertz argues that ethnographic research should be 'neither imprisoned within [the participants'] mental horizons . . . nor systematically deaf to the distinctive tonalities of their existence' (1999, p. 52). Recognizing that any researcher will always bring their own pre-judgements and understanding of the world to their research means that rather than seeking to resolve the tensions in my own relationship to the research, I instead practised reflexivity. In writing an account of the project and the learnings I have drawn from it, I have been careful to 'write myself in', to acknowledge my own position and the way that this shaped the research. This transparency is essential to good practice within ethnography and means that anyone reading this research can see both its gifts and its limitations in reflecting on the relevance it may have for their own situation.

The research process

As mentioned in Chapter 1, this project consists of 16 semi-structured life story interviews accompanied by ethnographic participant observation, which involves 'direct observation and experience' in order to access 'the meanings of human existence as seen from the standpoint of insiders' (Jorgensen, 1989, pp. 14–23). I gathered data as a participant observer in the context of the interviews over time in my role developing the national Network as an employee of The Message Trust, and in my local involvement in a neighbourhood and church community.

To identify interviewees I adopted a purposive sampling strategy, which is different from a representative sample in that, rather than focusing on a group that reflects the demographic characteristics of the community as a whole, it focuses on a 'relevant range' of criteria (Mason, 2002, pp. 123–24; May, 2011, p. 100; Punch, 2014, p. 164): in this case, the experiences of interactions either as, or with, Eden team members and an identification with the language of transformation. Alongside this I gave attention to gender, age, length of time involved with Eden and, for the team members, their church affiliation, aiming for a diverse participant group, broadly reflective of the Eden Network as it was at that time and the communities represented in the study. All of my interviewees agreed to take part in the study voluntarily and gave informed consent. They were made aware that the study was independent of the Eden Network and that they could withdraw at any time, even after the interview if they did not want their interview to be part of the final study.

Life-story interviewing is an approach that focuses on the narrative of the story-teller (Bold, 2012, pp. 97–8). I began each interview by inviting the interviewee to 'tell me a bit of your personal story', and allowed this to become the main part of the conversation; I followed up with questions about their involvement with Eden if necessary. This approach enabled me to hear participants' own accounts of their lives, the events and the different people who had been significant in their stories.

It is important to acknowledge that these interviews are co-constructed stories. This means that participants told their stories in a way that was particular to that day, time and place as well as their relationship with me and their expectations of the interview. On another day, or with a different interviewer, they may have told their story differently. My role as an employee of the Eden Network meant that I had a relationship with the Eden team members and some of the community members I interviewed, who were familiar with me facilitating training and reflection for Eden teams. I approached additional community member participants through Eden team leaders, and in these cases I was seen both as a friend of the Eden team leader and as a staff member of the Eden Network.

There is inevitably an imbalance of power between a researcher and interviewee, further complicated in this research by differences in class and my positional power as an employee of the Eden Network. There was the potential for participants, particularly those with whom I did not have a pre-existing relationship, to feel inhibited or to say what they felt was expected of them. In order to address this I hoped to help participants feel more at ease and in control by inviting them to choose the location of their interviews (Clark-King, 2003, p. 19). I met with most participants in their own homes, although some suggested a local church or a friend's house. Two community member participants did volunteer their thanks to Eden in the course of the interview, but these comments were offered as asides or at the very end. Starting the conversation by inviting them to tell their 'life story' meant that community member participants reflected on the changes they had seen in their lives, and Eden teams appeared as characters in these stories to a greater or lesser extent.

Some of my community member participants were under 18 and others I considered vulnerable, using the sociologist Hannah Farrimond's definition of vulnerable groups as those 'traditionally marginalised, disadvantaged or stigmatised' and 'groups living in dangerous or impoverished structural environments or engaging in risky behaviours' (2013, p. 159). Researchers have an ethical responsibility towards their participants and so I prepared to be sensitive to how these participants might engage with the interview process and flexible in responding to them (Gregory, 2003, p. 3). One interview was in fact cut short as the participant was having a difficult day and felt she would prefer not to continue, although she agreed for the shortened interview to remain a part of the project. For the two of my community member participants who were under the age of 16, parental consent was obtained for them to take part. In one case the participant's mum stayed in the room with us during the interview, looking after a younger sibling. While this will have undoubtedly affected the stories that this 16-year-old chose to share, I considered that it was important to enable the participation of young people even in this limited sense.

Many, if not most, of my interviews contained the discussion of issues that I considered 'sensitive', defined as subjects that are not usually part of everyday conversation, including criminal or illegal activity, and personal topics that may cause distress (Farrimond, 2013, p. 163). Some interviewees did become emotional at times and I sought to exercise my duty of care by giving them the space they needed and the option to discontinue the conversation if they chose. My approach was to listen actively and empathetically, gently facilitating their telling of their story. Despite the vulnerability of the process, in all cases participants remained committed to participate, and even alongside stories of great pain there were narratives of hope and resilience.

Ensuring anonymity for my participants required care as the Eden Network is a distinct group with a strong culture of sharing stories both within the Network and publicly. Team members might be identified within their teams, and community members may be identified by team members in their neighbourhoods. Therefore I adopted the researcher Cory Labanow's approach, limiting the amount of personal detail given for each participant (2009, p. 41). I have given each of my participants a pseudonym, and have offered additional detail only where relevant and where it cannot lead to their being identified. I have used geographic regions rather than specific community locations and I refer to the two Eden team leader participants simply as team members.

I analysed the interview data by taking a narrative approach to thematic analysis and 'open coding' (Bold, 2012, p. 130). My aim was to discern insight about the topic both from the content of the story (what happens) and from the way the story is constructed (what is included or missed out). Having transcribed the interviews, I looked at them as stories, noting the narrative arc, the characters and plot lines in the story. I then used thematic analysis to read the interviews alongside notes from my participant observation, coding the issues or questions that were significant for my participants. Some of these resonated with the questions that had prompted this research whereas others were unexpected and surprising.

While I anticipated that being exposed to different perspectives would be significant in enabling life change, the importance of an affirmation of personhood was new to me. As personhood and agency came to the fore throughout the process of analysis, I read my interview transcripts, looking specifically for agentic language – the use of 'I' in their stories – to understand how my interviewees perceived their own agency. This built up a picture for each person of how they understand their lives – whether they see themselves as the main 'actor', or whether they perceive life events to have happened to them or to have been initiated by someone else. For example, community member Margaret showed a strong sense of agency in her life change. In our conversation, as she emphasized the importance of relationships with team members, I asked her a follow-on question. Here is our exchange:

Are there any things other than the relationships that have been important in how you've actually made that change?

Just myself. The main thing is I've got to change myself. I've got to. I've got to stand on my own two feet and make my legs stronger. So I know I can do it and I'm determined to do it . . .

Central to my practical theological approach is to be open to the insight contained in the everyday experiences of ordinary people that might point towards the activity of God. Data analysis was a kind of creative conversation between the experiences of my participants, my participant observation and other relevant fields of knowledge, in this case the Christian tradition, academic work on pastoral care and sociology of religion.

How useful is practical theological research?

It is helpful to be clear about what kind of knowledge practical theological research can generate. My material cannot give you a full account of what every person in the Eden Network has felt about their mission. I cannot tell you the percentage of Eden team members who have wrestled with their theology. That was not my aim. This methodological approach prioritizes the subjectivity of participants' narratives above generalizable 'facts', focusing on understanding the way it is for the people I have encountered. This means that my conclusions cannot be seen as 'normative', offering a universal account of all evangelicals or all incarnational urban mission (Bold, 2012, p. 5). Missional pastoral care is my own interpretation of the data; as Geertz puts it: it is 'something made' (1973, p. 15). This raises issues of validity and transferability: how useful is this kind of knowledge?

This project needs to be evaluated first on its capacity to bring insight and clarity to the practice of incarnational urban mission. In part, this involves accurately holding up a mirror to urban mission, reflecting the missional practices observed back to those engaged in them. But it also brings these practices into conversation with broader theoretical frameworks (Geertz, 1973, p. 17). In this research I have generated a 'thick description' of the ministry practice of the Eden Network that goes beyond the physical, observable events of a situation, setting them within the 'ideas, constructs of thought and behaviour' of participants in order to understand what the events mean to them (Geertz, 1973, pp. 6–7). While the outcomes may be tentative, this approach enables me to account for the way in which individuals construct 'spiritual and self-identities' and the implications of this for mission practice (Ganzevoort, 2011, pp. 223–4).

One acknowledged limitation of this programme of research is that it was majority white, with only one black participant, and all but one of the urban communities represented were also majority white. Clearly, this is not representative of the diversity in Britain's urban spaces. The theologian Anthony Reddie articulates the way in which 'whiteness' is normative in our society – it becomes invisible because it is assumed to be the norm in many contexts (2018, pp. 6–7). For example, a white person describing a black person might say they are young, old, male or female but would most likely also include that they are black. But when a white person describes another white person it is rare for whiteness to be part of their initial description unless it is specifically to distinguish them from other members of a group. A black person is seen as a black person, a white person is simply seen as a person. The 'normalness' of whiteness is not just about population numbers, it is also about privilege. Ethnic minorities are consistently under-represented within the most senior and powerful sectors of British society, and their life chances in relation to education, employment and health are significantly restricted compared to the white population (Eddo-Lodge, 2018, pp. 67–72). Raised in a context of white normativity, it takes commitment to take off these blinkers in order to acknowledge the privilege that comes with being white in UK society.

With this structural prejudice in mind, I acknowledge the potential for whiteness to be normative in this research. Naming it is important. My own whiteness, and that of the majority of my participants, does not invalidate this research but it is vital to see it in that context, as a book about majority-white evangelical mission among (mostly) majority-white urban communities. My hope is that it will provide points of resonance for people of different ethnicities engaged in mission, and for those engaged in mission in strongly multicultural contexts, but their experiences and perspectives will be different and I welcome the opportunity to learn from them. The work of Anthony Reddie along with others listed in the Further Reading section provides a fruitful starting point for engagement with broader cultural perspectives on urban mission.

Geertz describes the process of engaging the local detail of ethnographic research with global structures or concepts as 'dialectical' movement, a cyclical process in which they begin to explain one another (1999, pp. 61–2). This is what I have done with Gerkin's work in pastoral care, with those writing about mission and marginality, and with the theologians and sociologists considering contemporary evangelicalism. Missional pastoral care will never be the final word on mission, but it offers insight into how mission has worked in one particular time and place, and how that connects and contributes to the learning of those in other specific contexts. Throughout the research process I have used my developing ideas in discussions with mission practitioners, and since completing the work I have explored missional pastoral care as a mode of missional living, along with its theological frameworks, with people in many different settings. These ideas have been warmly received by those who have found resonance with them in varied missional contexts. The knowledge generated by this piece of research functions to *clarify* the events occurring in relationships between mission practitioners and urban community members and to draw out their points of engagement with theoretical conceptions of evangelicalism, pastoral care and mission. Where it resonates with people involved in mission, and where it can offer focus for reflection, prayer and listening (to God and to those we may have 'othered'), it has something to contribute to our understanding of God and God's mission in the world.

Bibliography

Astley, J., 2002, *Ordinary Theology: Looking, Listening and Learning in Theology*, Aldershot: Ashgate.

Atherton, J., 2014, *Challenging Religious Studies: The Wealth, Wellbeing and Inequalities of Nations*, London: SCM Press.

Bailey, G., 2010, 'Entire Sanctification and Theological Method', in T. Greggs, ed., *New Perspectives for Evangelical Theology*, London: Routledge, pp. 63–74.

Baker, C., 2009, *The Hybrid Church in the City*, London: SCM Press.

Barclay, O., 1997, *Evangelicalism in Britain, 1935–95: A Personal Sketch*, London: IVP.

Bebbington, D. W., 1989, *Evangelicalism in Modern Britain*, London: Unwin Hyman.

Bebbington, D. W., 2010, 'Evangelicalism', in D. A. Fergusson, ed., *The Blackwell Companion to Nineteenth-Century Theology*, London: Wiley-Blackwell, pp. 235–50.

Berry, J., 2014, 'A Safe Space for Healing: Boundaries, Power and Vulnerability in Pastoral Care', *Theology & Sexuality*, 20(3), pp. 203–13.

Bevans, S. B. and Schroeder, R. P., 2011, *Prophetic Dialogue: Reflections on Christian Mission Today*, New York: Orbis Books.

Bialecki, J., 2009, 'The Bones Restored to Life: Dialogue and Dissemination in the Vineyard's Dialectic of Text and Presence', in J. Bielo, ed., *The Social Life of Scriptures: Cross-cultural Perspectives on Biblicism*, London: Rutgers University Press, pp. 136–56.

Bielo, J., 2008, 'On the Failure of "Meaning": Bible Reading in the Anthropology of Christianity', *Culture and Religion*, 9(1), pp. 1–21.

Bielo, J., 2011a, *Emerging Evangelicals: Faith, Modernity and the Desire for Authenticity*, New York: New York University Press.

Bielo, J., 2011b, 'Purity, Danger and Redemption: Notes on Urban Missional Evangelicals', *American Ethnologist*, 38(2), pp. 267–80.

Biggar, N., 2011, *Behaving in Public: How to Do Christian Ethics*, Grand Rapids, MI: Eerdmans.

Bold, C., 2012, *Using Narrative in Research*, London: Sage.

Booth, W., 1890, *In Darkest England and the Way Out*, Virginia: IndyPublish.com.

Bosch, D. J., 2011, *Transforming Mission: Paradigm Shifts in Theology of Mission*, 2nd edn, New York: Orbis Books.

Brown, B., 2013, *Daring Greatly*, London: Portfolio Penguin.

Cartledge, M. J., 2004, 'Charismatic Theology: Approaches and Themes', *Journal of Beliefs and Values*, 25(2), pp. 177–90.

Chaplin, J., 2015, 'Evangelicalism and the Language(s) of the Common Good', in N. Sagovski and P. McGrail, eds, *Together for the Common Good: Towards a National Conversation*, London: SCM Press, pp. 91–106.

Clark-King, E., 2003, *Sacred Hearts: Feminist Theology Interrogated by the Voices of Working-Class Women*, Lancaster: Lancaster University Press.

Coghlan, D. and Brannick, T., 2005, *Doing Action Research in Your Own Organisation*, 2nd edn, London: Sage.

Coleman, S., 2000, *The Globalisation of Charismatic Christianity*, Cambridge: Cambridge University Press.

Crites, S., 1971, 'The Narrative Quality of Experience', *Journal of the American Academy of Religion*, 39(3), pp. 291–311.

Crossan, J. D., 1988, *The Dark Interval: Towards a Theology of Story*, Salem, OR: Polebridge Press.

Crossan, J. D., 1992, *In Parables: The Challenge of the Historical Jesus*, Salem, OR: Polebridge Press.

Davey, A., 2001, *Urban Christianity and Global Order*, London: SPCK.

Davies, M., 2018, 'Why I'm still an evangelical in the age of Trump', Available at: www.ft.com/content/dfc42aba-d71e-11e8-a854-33d6f82e62f8 (accessed 30 May 2019).

Donovan, V., 2001, *Christianity Rediscovered*, 3rd edn, London: SCM Press.

Drane, J., 2000, *The McDonaldization of the Church*, London: Darton Longman and Todd.

Eddo-Lodge, R., 2018, *Why I'm No Longer Talking to White People About Race*, London: Bloomsbury.

Engelke, M., 2013, *God's Agents: Biblical Publicity in Contemporary England*, London: University of California Press.

Evangelical Alliance, 2011, *21st Century Evangelicals*, London: Evangelical Alliance.

Evangelical Alliance, 2012, *21st Century Evangelicals: Confidently Sharing the Gospel?*, London: Evangelical Alliance.

Farrimond, H., 2013, *Doing Ethical Research*, Basingstoke: Palgrave Macmillan.

Fox, M., 1983, *Original Blessing*, Santa Fe, NM: Bear & Co.

Fox, M., Martin, P. and Green, G., 2007, *Doing Practitioner Research*, London: Sage.

France, R. T. and McGrath, A. E., 1993, *Evangelical Anglicans: Their Role and Influence in the Church Today*, London: SPCK.

Francis, L., 2011, 'Religion and Happiness: Perspectives from the Psychology of Religion, Positive Psychology and Empirical Theology', in J. Atherton, F. Graham and I. Steedman, eds, *The Practices of Happiness: Political Economy, Religion and Wellbeing*, London: Routledge, pp. 113–24.

Frost, M. and Hirsch, A., 2013, *The Shaping of Things to Come: Innovation and Mission for the 21st-Century Church*, 2nd edn, Grand Rapids, MI: Baker Books.

Ganzevoort, R., 2010, 'Minding the Wisdom of Ages: Narrative Approaches in Pastoral Care for the Elderly', *Practical Theology*, 3(3), pp. 331–40.

Ganzevoort, R., 2011, 'Narrative Approaches', in B. J. Miller-McLemore, ed., *The Wiley-Blackwell Companion to Practical Theology*, Chichester: Wiley-Blackwell, pp. 214–23.

Garnett, J. et al., 2007, *Redefining Christian Britain: Post 1945 Perspectives*, London: SCM Press.

Geertz, C., 1973, *The Interpretation of Cultures*, New York: Basic Books.

Geertz, C., 1999, '"From the Native's Point of View": On the Nature of Anthropological Understanding', in R. T. McCutcheon, ed., *The Insider/Outsider Problem in the Study of Religion: A Reader*, London: Continuum, pp. 50–63.

Gerkin, C. V., 1984, *The Living Human Document*, Nashville, TN: Abingdon Press.

Gerkin, C. V., 1986, *Widening the Horizons: Pastoral Responses to a Fragmented Society*, Philadelphia, PA: Westminster Press.

Gerkin, C. V., 1997, *An Introduction to Pastoral Care,* Nashville, TN: Abingdon Press.

Glasser, A., 1985, 'The Evolution of Evangelical Mission Theology since World War II', *International Bulletin of Missionary Research*, 9(1), Retrieved from ATLA Religion Database with ATLASerials database, pp. 9–13.

Goodhart, D., 2017, *The Road to Somewhere: The Populist Revolt and the Future of Politics*, London: C. Hurst & Co.

Graham, E., 2011, 'The "Virtuous Circle": Religion and the Practices of Happiness', in J. Atherton, E. Graham and I. Steedman, eds, *The Practices of Happiness: Political Economy, Religion and Wellbeing*, London: Routledge, pp. 224–34.

Graham, E., 2013, 'Is Practical Theology a Form of "Action Research"?', *International Journal of Practical Theology*, 17(1), pp. 148–78.

Graham, E. and Lowe, S., 2009, *What Makes a Good City? Public Theology and the Urban Church*, London: Darton, Longman and Todd.

Green, L., 2009, *Let's Do Theology: Resources for Contextual Theology*, London: Mowbray.

Greggs, T. E., 2010, *New Perspectives for Evangelical Theology*, London: Routledge.

Gregory, I., 2003, *Ethics in Research*, London: Continuum.

Grenz, S. J., 1994, *Theology for the Community of God*, Nashville, TN: Broadman and Holman.

Grinnell, A., 2018, 'Poverty Truth in Leeds', in *Crucible: Truth and Faith in Public Life*, July 2018, pp. 42–50.

Guest, M., 2007, *Evangelical Identity and Contemporary Culture*, Milton Keynes: Paternoster.

Guest, M., 2012, 'Keeping the End in Mind: "Left Behind", the Apocalypse and the Evangelical Imagination', *Literature and Theology*, 26(4 Apocalypse Now and Then), pp. 474–88.

Hanley, L., 2007, *Estates: An Intimate History*, London: Granta Books.

Hanley, L., 2017, *Respectable: The Experience of Class*, London: Penguin.

Harris, B., 2008, 'Beyond Bebbington: The Quest for Evangelical Identity in a Post-modern Era', *Churchman*, 122(3), pp. 201–19.

Herrick, V., 1997, *Limits of Vulnerability: Exploring a Kenotic Model for Pastoral Ministry*, Cambridge: Grove Books.

Hiebert, P. and Hiebert Meneses, E., 1995, *Incarnational Ministry*, Grand Rapids, MI: Baker Books.

Hilborn, D., 2019, *What Is an Evangelical?*, available at: www.eauk.org/about-us/how-we-work/tag/what-is-an-evangelical (accessed 15 May 2019).

Holmes, S. R., 2007, 'British (and European) Evangelical Theologies', in T. Larsen and D. J. Treier, eds, *The Cambridge Companion to Evangelical Theology*, Cambridge: Cambridge University Press, pp. 241–58.

Hufford, D. J., 1999, 'The Scholarly Voice and the Personal Voice: Reflexivity in Belief Studies', in R. T. McCutcheon, ed., *The Insider/Outsider Problem in the Study of Religion: A Reader*, London: Continuum, pp. 294–310.

Hunt, S., 2005, 'The Alpha Programme: Charismatic Evangelism for the Contemporary Age', *Pneuma: The Journal of the Society for Pentecostal Studies*, 27(1), pp. 65–82.

Jagessar, M., 2009, 'Is Jesus the Only Way? Doing Black Christian God-talk in a Multi-Religious City (Birmingham, UK)', *Black Theology*, 7(2), pp. 200–25.

Jantzen, G. M., 1998, *Becoming Divine: Towards a Feminist Philosophy of Religion*, Manchester: Manchester University Press.

Jorgensen, D. L., 1989, *Participant Observation: A Methodology for Human Studies*, London: Sage.

Kahneman, D., 2011, *Thinking Fast and Slow*, London: Penguin.

Kuhn, T. S., 1996, *The Structure of Scientific Revolutions*, 3rd edn, Chicago: Chicago University Press.

Kuhrt, J., 2010, 'Going Deeper Together: Resisting Tribal Theology', in A. Davey, ed., *Crossover City*, London: Mowbray, pp. 14–21.

Kvale, S., 2007, *Doing Interviews*, London: Sage.

Labanow, C., 2009, *Evangelicalism and the Emerging Church*, Farnham: Ashgate.

Lambert, S., 2013, *A Christian Perspective on Attention, Awareness and Mindfulnes*, available at: www.mindandsoulfoundation.org/ Articles/339737/Mind_and_Soul/Articles/A_Christian_perspective. aspx (accessed 30 May 2019).

Lancey, R., 2012, 'Success or Failure?', in M. Wilson, *Concrete Faith*, Manchester: The Message Trust, pp. 81–4.

Larsen, T., 2007, 'Defining and Locating Evangelicalism', in T. Larsen and D. J. Treier, eds, *The Cambridge Companion to Evangelical Theology*, Cambridge: Cambridge University Press, pp. 1–14.

Linge, D. E., 1976, 'Editor's Introduction', in D. E. Linge, ed., *Philosophical Hermeneutics*, London: University of California Press, pp. xi–lv.

Luhrmann, T. M., 2004, 'Metakinesis: How God becomes Intimate in Contemporary U.S. Christianity', *American Anthropologist*, New Series, 106(3), pp. 518–28.

Lynch, G., 2002, *After Religion: Generation X and the Search for Meaning*, London: Darton, Longman and Todd.

Marsden, G., 1984, *Evangelicalism and Modern America*, Grand Rapids, MI: Eerdmans.

Mason, J., 2002, *Qualitative Researching*, 2nd edn, London: Sage.

May, T., 2011, *Social Research: Issues, Methods and Process*, 4th edn, Maidenhead: Open University Press.

McGavran, D., 1955, *The Bridges of God: A Study in the Strategy of Missions*, London: World Dominion Press.

McGrath, A. E., 1995, *Evangelicalism and the Future of Christianity*, Downers Grove, IL: InterVarsity Press.

McLaren, B., 2006, *A Generous Orthodoxy*, Grand Rapids, MI: Zondervan.

McLaren, B., 2007, *Everything Must Change*, Nashville, TN: Thomas Nelson.

McNiff, J., 2000, *Action Research in Organisations*, London: Routledge.

Newbigin, L., 1995, *The Open Secret: An Introduction to the Theology of Mission*, rev. edn, Grand Rapids, MI: Eerdmans.

Office for National Statistics, 2019, *Health state life expectancies by national deprivation deciles, England and Wales: 2014–2016*, available at: www.ons.gov.uk/peoplepopulationandcommunity/

healthandsocialcare/healthinequalities/bulletins/healthstatelife
expectanciesbyindexofmultipledeprivationimd/englandandwales
2014to2016.

Olson, R. E., 2005, *The SCM Press A–Z of Evangelical Theology*, London: SCM Press.

Paloutzian, R. F., 2005, 'Religious Conversion and Spiritual Transformation: A Meaning-System Analysis', in R. F. Paloutzian and C. L. Park, eds, *Handbook of the Psychology of Religion and Spirituality*, London: Guilford Press, pp. 331–47.

Pears, M., 2013, 'Urban Expression: Convictional Communities and Urban Social Justice', in A. Williams, J. Beaumont and P. Cloke, eds, *Working Faith: Faith-based Organisations and Urban Social Justice*, Milton Keynes: Paternoster, pp. 85–110.

Pears, M., 2016, 'Place and Marginality: The Formation of Redemptive Places', in P. Cloke and M. Pears, eds, *Mission in Marginal Places: The Theory*, Milton Keynes: Paternoster, pp. 33–56.

Punch, K. F., 2014, *Introduction to Social Research: Quantitative and Qualitative Approaches*, 3rd edn, London: Sage.

Raleigh, V., 2019, *What is happening to life expectancy in the UK?*, available at: www.kingsfund.org.uk/publications/whats-happening-life-expectancy-uk?gclid=EAIaIQobChMIkITdgI7t3wIVq7ftCh2C7 gXaEAAYASAAEgKNOvD_BwE.

Reddie, A., 2018, 'Now You See Me Now You Don't: Subjectivity, Blackness and Difference in Practical Theology in Britain Post-brexit', *Practical Theology*, 11(1), pp. 4–16.

Redfield Jamison, K., 2004, *Exuberance: The Passion for Life*, New York: Random House.

Rooms, N., 2015, 'Missional Gift-Giving: A Practical Theology Investigation into what Happens when Churches Give Away "Free" Gifts for the Sake of Mission', *Practical Theology*, 8(2), pp. 99–111.

Ruddick, A., 2018, 'Flourishing and Ambiguity in UK Urban Mission', in C. R. Baker and E. Graham, eds, *Theology for Changing Times*, London: SCM Press, pp. 143–57.

Scharen, C. and Vigen, A. M., 2011, *Ethnography as Christian Theology and Ethics*, London: Continuum.

Siegel, D., 2011, *Mindsight*, 2nd edn, London: Oneworld.

Skeggs, B., 1997, *Formations of Class and Gender: Becoming Respectable*, London: Sage.

Smith, C., 1998, *American Evangelicalism: Embattled and Thriving*, London: University of Chicago Press.

Smith, C., 2000, *Christian America? What Evangelicals Really Want*, Berkeley, CA: University of California Press.

Smith, C., 2012, *The Bible Made Impossible: Why Biblicism is not a Truly Evangelical Reading of Scripture*, Grand Rapids, MI: Brazos Press.

Smith, G., 2017, 'Evangelical Social Action in the UK', *Crucible, the Journal of Christian Social Ethics*, October, pp. 25–37.

Smith, M., 2008, 'Introduction: British Evangelical Identities: Locating the Discussion', in M. Smith, ed., *British Evangelical Identities Past and Present Volume 1: Aspects of the History and Sociology of Evangelicalism in Britain and Ireland*, Milton Keynes: Paternoster.

Sremac, S., 2014, 'Faith, Hope, and Love: A Narrative Theological Analysis of Recovering Drug Addicts' Conversion Testimonies', *Practical Theology*, 7(1), pp. 34–49.

Stackhouse, J., 2002, *Evangelical Landscapes: Facing Critical Issues of the Day*, Grand Rapids, MI: Baker Academic.

Stoddart, E., 2012, 'Current Thinking in Pastoral Theology', *The Expository Times*, 123(7), pp. 323–33.

Strhan, A., 2012, 'Latour, Prepositions and the Instauration of Secularism', *Political Theology*, 13(2), pp. 200–16.

Strhan, A., 2013, 'Practising the Space Between: Embodying Belief as an Evangelical Anglican Student', *Journal of Contemporary Religion*, 28(2), pp. 225–39.

Strhan, A., 2015, *Aliens and Strangers? The Struggle for Coherence in the Everyday Lives of Evangelicals*, Oxford: Oxford University Press.

Swinton, J., 2001, *Spirituality and Mental Health Care*, London: Jessica Kingsley.

Swinton, J., 2011, 'Who is the God We Worship? Theologies of Disability; Challenges and New Possibilities', *International Journal of Practical Theology*, 14(2), pp. 273–307.

Swinton, J. and Mowat, H., 2006, *Practical Theology and Qualitative Research*, London: SCM Press.

Swinton, J. and Pattison, S., 2010, 'Moving Beyond Clarity: Towards a Thin, Vague, and Useful Understanding of Spirituality in Nursing Care', *Nursing Philosophy*, 11(4), pp. 226–37.

Taylor, J. V., 1972, *The Go-Between God: The Holy Spirit and the Christian Mission*, London: SCM Press.

Thacker, J., 2010, 'Book Reviews', *Ecclesiology*, 6(2), pp. 213–57.

Thompson, A., 2010, 'Eden Fitton Hill: Demonstrating and Becoming in Oldham', in A. Davey, ed., *Crossover City: Resources for Urban Mission and Transformation*, London: Mowbray, pp. 120–24.

Thompson, A., 2012, 'Holy Sofas: Transformational Encounters between Evangelical Christians and Post-Christendom Urban Communities', *Practical Theology*, 5(1), pp. 47–64.

Tidball, D., 2005, 'The Bible in Evangelical Spirituality', in P. H. Ballard and S. Holmes, eds, *The Bible in Pastoral Practice*, London: Darton, Longman and Todd, pp. 258–74.

Tomlinson, D., 1995, *The Post-Evangelical*, London: SPCK.

Veling, T., 2005, *Practical Theology*, New York: Orbis Books.

Warner, R., 2007, *Reinventing English Evangelicalism 1966–2001*, Milton Keynes: Paternoster.

Wells, S., 2015, *Nazareth Manifesto: Being with God*, Chichester: Wiley-Blackwell.

Wier, A., 2013, 'Tensions in Charismatic-Evangelical Urban Practice: Towards a Practical Charismatic-Evangelical Urban Social Ethic', unpublished doctoral dissertation, Chester: University of Chester.

Wilson, M., 2012, *Concrete Faith*, Manchester: Message Publications.

Wolterstorff, N., 1983, *Until Justice and Peace Embrace*, Grand Rapids, MI: Eerdmans.

Wright, T., 2005, *Scripture and the Authority of God*, London: SPCK.

Zahl, S., 2010, 'Reformation Pessimism or Pietist Personalism? The Problem of the Holy Spirit in Evangelical Theology', in T. Greggs, ed., *New Perspectives for Evangelical Theology*, London: Routledge, pp. 78–92.

Further Reading

In addition to the Bibliography, you might find the following books helpful if you want to pursue some of the themes in this book.

Mission in urban or marginalized communities

Cloke, P. and Pears, M. (eds), *Mission in Marginal Places* series. Includes *The Theory*, 2016; *The Praxis*, 2016; and *The Stories*, 2019, Milton Keynes: Paternoster.

Davey, A., 2001, *Urban Christianity and Global Order*, London: SPCK.

Davey, A. (ed.), 2010, *Crossover City*, London: Mowbray.

Green, L., 2009, *Let's Do Theology, Resources for Contextual Theology*, London: Mowbray.

Hayes, John B., 2007, *Sub-Merge: Living Deep in a Shallow World*, Grand Rapids, MI: Baker House.

Heuertz, C. and Pohl, C., 2010, *Friendship at the Margins: Discovering Mutuality in Service and Mission*, Downers Grove, IL: InterVarsity Press.

Keeble, P., 2017, *Mission With: Something out of the Ordinary*, Manchester: Instant Apostle.

Lane, C., 2017, *Ordinary Miracles, Mess, Meals and Meeting Jesus in Unexpected Places*, Manchester: Instant Apostle.

Morisy, Ann, 2004, *Journeying Out: A New Approach to Christian Mission*, London: Continuum.

Murray, Stuart, 2004, *Post-Christendom: Church and Mission in a Strange New World*, Milton Keynes: Paternoster.

Shannahan, C., 2010, *Voices from the Borderland: Re-imagining Cross-cultural Urban Theology in the Twenty First Century*, London: Equinox.

Sparks, P., Soerens, T. and Friesen, Dwight J., 2014, *The New Parish: How Neighborhood Churches Are Transforming Mission, Discipleship and Community*, Downers Grove, IL: InterVarsity Press.

Wells, S., 2017, *Incarnational Ministry: Being with the Church*, Grand Rapids, MI: Eerdmans.

Broader cultural perspectives on urban mission and theology

Beckford, R., 2004, *God and the Gangs: An Urban Toolkit for Those Who Won't Be Bought Out, Sold Out or Scared Out*, London: Darton, Longman and Todd.

Beckford, R., 2006, *Jesus Dub: Theology, Music and Social Change*, London: Routledge.

Cone, James H., 2010, *A Black Theology of Liberation*, 40th anniversary edition, Maryknoll, NY: Orbis Books.

Jagessar, Michael N., 2009, 'Is Jesus the Only Way? Doing Black Christian God-talk in a Multi-religious City (Birmingham, UK)', *Black Theology*, 7(2) (2009), pp. 200–25.

Jagessar, Michael N. and Reddie, Anthony G., 2007, *Post-Colonial Black British Theology – New Textures and Themes*, Peterborough: Epworth.

Reddie, Anthony G., 2012, *Black Theology*, London: SCM Press.

Community development and strengths-based approaches to Christian community engagement

Andrews, D., 2006, *Compassionate Community Work*, Carlisle: Piquant Editions.

Block, P., Brueggemann, W. and McKnight, J., 2016, *An Other Kingdom: Departing the Consumer Culture*, Hoboken, NJ: John Wiley & Sons.

Boyle, D. and Harris, M., 2009, *The Challenge of Co-Production*, London: Nesta.

Broad, R., 2015, *People, Places, Possibilities: Progress on Local Area Coordination in England and Wales*, Sheffield: The Centre for Welfare Reform.

Eckley, B., Ruddick, A. and Walker, R., 2015, *Fullness of Life Together: Reimagining Christian Engagement in our Communities*, London: Livability and Church Urban Fund.

Gordon, W. and Perkins, J., 2013, *Making Neighborhoods Whole: A Handbook for Christian Community Development*, Downers Grove, IL: InterVarsity Press.

Hanley, L., 2007, *Estates: An Intimate History*, London: Granta Books.

Lupton, R. D., 2012, *Toxic Charity: How Churches and Charities Hurt Those They Help and How to Reverse It*, San Francisco, CA: HarperOne.

Mather, M., 2018, *Having Nothing, Possessing Everything: Finding Abundant Communities in Unexpected Places*, Grand Rapids, MI: Eerdmans.

McKnight, J. and Block, P., 2012, *The Abundant Community: Awakening the Power of Families and Neighborhoods*, Oakland, CA: Berrett-Koehler Publishers.

Ruddick, A. and Eckley, B., 2016, *Building Kingdom Communities: The Prophetic Role of the Church in Community Engagement*, London: Livability and Church Urban Fund.

Wells, S., Rook, R. and Barclay, D., 2017, *For Good: The Church and the Future of Welfare*, Norwich: Canterbury Press.

Religion and well-being

Atherton, J., Baker, C. and Reader, J., 2011, *Christianity and the New Social Order*, London: SPCK.

Atherton, J., Graham, E. and Steedman, I. (eds), 2011, *The Practices of Happiness: Political Economy, Religion and Wellbeing*, London: Routledge.

Ruddick, A., 2018, 'Flourishing and Ambiguity in UK Urban Mission', in C. R. Baker and E. Graham (eds), *Theology for Changing Times*, London: SCM Press, pp. 143–57.

Index